# Be YOU, NO FILTER

# Be YOU, NO FILTER

## How to Love Yourself and Stay #SocialMediaStrong

**LATASHA BLACKMOND**

Copyright © 2020 by Latasha Blackmond

All rights reserved. No part of this book may be used or reproduced in any manner whatsoever including Internet usage, without written permission of the author.

Book design by Maureen Cutajar
www.gopublished.com

ISBN: 978-0-578-61973-6

*I dedicate this book to my daughter, Alana who is a constant reminder that there is good in this world.*

*To my tribe that keeps me accountable every day with laughs,stories, and tears we'll take to the grave.*

*And to my 16-year-old self, the journey will have twists and turns, heartaches, doubts and seem confusing at times. But it all will lead to an abundance of love and light. Learn the lesson in it all.*

# Contents

| | | |
|---|---|---|
| INTRODUCTION | | 1 |
| CHAPTER ONE | Pick Yourself | 5 |
| CHAPTER TWO | Throw Comparison in the Trash | 23 |
| CHAPTER THREE | Know You Are More Than A Body | 35 |
| CHAPTER FOUR | Never Stop Growing | 53 |
| CHAPTER FIVE | Don't Do Life Alone | 65 |
| CHAPTER SIX | Setting Boundaries | 75 |
| CHAPTER SEVEN | Handle Your Heart with Care | 85 |
| CHAPTER EIGHT | Setting the Right Goals to Be a Better You | 99 |
| CHAPTER NINE | Change for the Better-and Forever | 105 |
| CONCLUSION | | 113 |

# INTRODUCTION

Being a young woman in today's world isn't easy.

Every generation comes with its own set of challenges and pressures. I had mine, and your grandmothers, mothers, aunties, and big sisters did too. But you have to contend with one thing that we did not. Something that, chances are, you can't avoid for long, no matter how hard you try. It's that thing you have a love/hate relationship with. It's that thing, I'm guessing, that causes you to constantly question yourself more than anything else.

Social media.

Now, social media definitely has so many benefits. With the whole world at your fingertips, it is a tool you can use to explore just about anything and everything. It can open your mind and eyes to new things. You can meet people you may not otherwise have come into contact with and find out about new places to experience and travel to. You can get a glimpse into the lives of your favorite celebrities, find inspiration for fashion and makeup, and discover other women who are attending the schools you'd love to go to and who have the careers you dream about. Social media is an all-access pass to an entire world beyond your neighborhood and can take you literally anywhere you want to go.

But challenges come with all that access. With constant exposure to the entire universe, it can be easy to spend hours of your day, every day, just watching and studying people. We hop from Instagram to Snapchat to Twitter to Facebook to keep up with people we're interested in. And if you're like most women, you follow a lot of ladies just to keep up with every detail of their exciting lives. Their perfect hair, perfect skin, and perfect bodies come along with the package. We consume that content all day; it's like the air we breathe.

If you are constantly bombarded with images of girls and women who seem (notice I said *seem*) to have the makeup, clothes, booties, and boyfriends that every other woman in the world wants, it's easy to fall into the trap of doubting yourself. If you don't look like those women or have access to the same amount of money or attention, you begin to question your beauty, smile, intelligence, and all of the other wonderful qualities that make you special. You start to wonder if you are enough. You're not alone.

Every woman alive, young and old, has struggled with

self-esteem. I have been there, and I have days when I still am. The journey to womanhood is hard, and it is full of bumps and experiences and people that will shake your confidence. It can take a long time to get comfortable with yourself and develop a deep self-love that nothing and nobody can shake. But I am hoping that this book will help you avoid some of the headaches and heartaches that come when you allow outside influences to make you forget who you are.

This book contains the words I wish another woman in my life had shared with me. Yes, I figured out a lot of stuff on my own—about taking care of myself, getting through college, men, and eventually, even becoming a single mom. I learned hard lessons about loving myself and accepting myself, flaws and all, and embracing my beauty. I've been through many struggles that stemmed from not loving and accepting myself sooner. Now that I have a daughter, I often talk to her and my nieces about their perceptions of themselves. What I know is that so many girls find it hard to accept themselves as they are. Girls who look in the mirror and can't like what they see. Girls who allow the world to tell them who and what they should be.

That world you're seeing through the small screen of your smartphone is just a tiny bit of reality. I know it can be hard not to judge yourself based on what you see. But your ability to stay strong and enjoy social media for the entertainment that it is comes down to one thing: Loving Yourself.

At this time in your life, you should be loving yourself

more than you love anyone else. Now is the time to set your standards, to take care of yourself, and to establish a strong sense of self. You'll know what and who to allow in your life. You'll be able to walk away from situations and people who don't treat you well and aren't good for you. You will not tolerate disrespect. You won't be bothered by someone else's likes or hearts or favorites on a selfie they post. On most days, it won't matter to you if anyone tells you you're beautiful, smart, or special. You'll already know it for yourself. Their compliments are just a bonus.

So as you're reading this book, I want you to be prepared to think. As we move through these pages, I'll ask you to stop and ask yourself a few questions about how you feel. I want you to get a blank journal (you don't need to spend a lot of money on it), a notebook, or loose paper so you write out your answers to my questions and your thoughts about how you feel. This is important.

While we will talk a lot about social media, what we're going to talk about most is you. I want you to look within and start to see yourself differently. In this world of filtered photos and fake lives, I want you to get comfortable being the real you. I want you to try using your social media a little differently as you learn more about yourself and what makes you feel your best, every day. I want you to focus way more time on yourself, your life, and your goals than you do anything or anyone else.

If you finish this book knowing how to do that, I promise you'll be a much better YOU.

## CHAPTER ONE

### Pick Yourself

When I was young, we lived to play. I remember sitting in those hot classrooms in Brooklyn as summer approached, watching the clock as it *tick-tocked* until noon, which was lunchtime in elementary school and junior high. Lunch was okay, but we really wanted to get to recess. It was a big thing, and we all looked forward to it.

Usually, right after lunch, we would burst through the cafeteria doors like wild Chihuahuas, the security guards right behind us, yelling for us to slow down. We practically tripped over each other to get outside for thirty minutes that seemed like five. Until that whistle blew to force us back to class, we could do whatever we wanted. We were free, and there was nothing like it.

Just like everywhere else in the world, school was a divided place. If you looked around the schoolyard, you would see all these little groups scattered all over—the cliques who gathered together based on what they looked like, how popular they were, or what they were good at. Everyone wanted to be cool and stand out.

There were the boys who played basketball at the back of the schoolyard with just the rim (the net fell off years ago), and their sad attempts at crossovers. There were the girls who were the double-dutch mavericks, and they all would cheer the loudest for that one girl who could jump her butt off or turn the best. And then there were the pretty fly girls who wouldn't dare do anything sports-related, but they were huddled up too, wearing their Guess or Girbaud jeans, watching everyone else. No one wanted to be left out. We all wanted to be the one.

One of my fondest memories from that time was that whenever it rained, we'd have to stay inside the building and play games. Sometimes we'd be in the lunchroom, making beats by banging on the tables and spitting out rhymes, and our teachers would let us decide whether we wanted to play board games or cards or something as a group. Of all the games in the world, these Brooklyn kids would want to play "7-Up." It was simple. Everybody in the class would put their heads on their desks and close their eyes. We would all stick our thumbs up in the air, and the teacher would pick seven kids in the class to walk around. Those kids' jobs were to pick seven other students by touching their thumbs. When we opened our eyes, we had to guess who touched who.

It would be so quiet in the room that you could hear our hearts beating, if you listened hard enough. The nerves were on high as we waited impatiently to feel that anticipated touch. If a girl was making the rounds, you would know from the way she gently grazed your thumb to choose you. Boys were much rougher, practically knocking your thumb out of socket as they playfully raced on to pick the next person before time was up. Either way, you didn't care. When you felt that touch, it made your day. You felt like Popeye after eating his can of spinach. As the rules went, if you felt a touch, you would quickly put your thumb down. Anyone who was chosen was likely smiling in anticipation, even though no one else could see it. You couldn't wait to make it known that you had made the cut.

Eventually, we'd hear the teacher say, "Okay everyone, open your eyes!"

We all sat still, looking out of the corners of our eyes as, one by one, the kids who were selected had a chance to guess who else was chosen. Holding our giggles inside, we waited for the picks to be revealed.

For the kids who were always chosen by their friends, this was the fun part. For kids like me, who were rarely a part of the few, you couldn't wait for the humiliation to be over. It was just a stupid game, but to a young person, it meant something. I think "7-Up" was my first experience with anxiety.

Every time I wasn't picked, the disappointment came. And then the questions flooded my mind.

*Why didn't you pick me?*

*Am I not good enough?*

*Is it because my thumb has an extra curve on it?*

*Aren't I popular?*

The seven-year-old me was so traumatized that I wanted to flip over every desk in the classroom. I couldn't figure out what it was and what kept me from being chosen. Sure, in second grade, I was tall like a giraffe and my arms reached down to the middle of my knees, but that proved to be a positive, or so I thought. My size kept all my friends from getting picked on. I was their personal bodyguard. (Little did they know I was all bark and no bite.) I was a good friend, and I always cracked jokes. (Some things don't change. That's still me today.) I was likable, and I didn't understand why I was left out. I just wanted to belong. I wanted to be picked, not just in the game in class, but for everything that was considered popular. I wanted to be liked and accepted. Those early experiences shaped so many years that followed.

From ages seven to seventeen to my early twenties, I was always looking for acceptance and to be included. We all do. I spent a lot of those years feeling like I was on the outside looking in, questioning my value, and wanting desperately to be validated. At the time, I wondered if I was the only girl who felt that way. Now I know better. Every girl has wanted to fit in at some point in her life.

She's heard that inner voice that whispers there is something wrong with her if she does not belong. *Wanting* to be liked and included is not a bad thing; *needing* to be liked and wanted can be.

The need to be popular can become a drug. Attention is addictive. Being picked feels good. Whenever we are lucky enough to be one of a chosen few, it's exciting. It's like feeling butterflies fluttering in your belly when you smile at the boy you like, and he smiles back.

We're happy. We feel special. So we want that same feeling over and over again. We crave it. We start to chase it. And when we get it, life is great. Everything is right with our world. But what happens when the attention isn't there? That can cause our world to start crumbling around us.

Not receiving attention isn't a problem until we don't get it. That's when we start to feel bad about ourselves. We begin to question if we're good enough. We find ourselves wondering about our worth. This pattern of behavior is so dangerous. On the days when people love us, we're up. When they don't, we're down. It feels like an emotional rollercoaster—because it is. And to love ourselves the way we should, we have to get off the ride.

## Mommy, Do You Love Me

My mom always took such pride in how her children looked. Like any typical Latino and Panamanian parent, if her child didn't look good, she believed that the world would judge her. Her reputation as a mom was based on how clean and well-dressed her kids were, so she took our appearance seriously. Our hair was neat and perfect. Our clothes were clean and crisp. Our faces, elbows, and knees were always greased. No exceptions. She did not play—at all. Whenever we got ready to leave the house, we were inspected one by one, from head to toe.

"I don't want people to think we don't keep you looking nice," she always said in her thick Panamanian accent as she fussed over me and my sister, smoothing our hair and clipping in the last of the barrettes (they had to be those big ponytail holders with the balls on the end; for some strange reason, she thought every color in the rainbow should be in our hair), straightening our clothes, and, depending on how early it was in the day, licking her fingers to clean that little bit of morning crust in the corners of our eyes, that only a mother can spot from a mile away.

She didn't say it, but what she meant was, "Don't embarrass me!" We made sure we didn't. Whether our mom was home or not, we never left the house without looking our absolute best. Not only did I learn early on that my appearance mattered (the nicer I looked, the more attention and compliments I got), but I also figured out that I never wanted to let my mother down. I'll be honest, there were times when I thought she was crazy. But she was still my mom. Her love and approval were the most important things in the world to me. I didn't want to do anything to lose it.

Before there are classmates, friends, and boyfriends, there are mothers. Our parents are the first people to teach us what love looks like, or sometimes, what it doesn't. Without realizing it, they train us to believe that love is conditional and we have to earn it by always doing the right thing. I am just meeting you, but I bet that when you were a baby, whenever you did something well, like took your first steps or said your first words, your mom clapped with excitement. Then as you got older, you kept earning her praise by cleaning your room, getting good grades, and not doing anything to embarrass her in public.

If you were a "good girl," she was happy. You felt liked. You felt approved. You knew better than to talk too loudly, too much, or to misbehave in any way. You didn't want to do anything to risk losing her love.

In your mind, you're always asking the question, "Mommy, do you still love me?"

So what do you do? Anything and everything you can to be perfect.

Once our hearts and minds make the connection that perfection equals praise, or, on the other hand, that flaws equal rejection, that belief sticks to us in a way that is hard to shake. Rejection, especially when we experience it early in life as little girls, is hard to overcome. The effects show up in different ways too. If we've been told all our lives that we won't be loved anymore if we do something wrong, we may:

- Do everything we can not to offend anyone, so we don't express our opinions.
- Be afraid to ruffle any feathers, so we always go along with the crowd, even when it feels wrong or it's not what we want to do.
- Act shy and become a chameleon that blends in with whoever is popular or the person we want to impress.
- Not trust our feelings and ideas, so constantly ask people for their opinions.
- Feel that we'd rather stay home than go out if we don't feel pretty that day.
- Become obsessed with how we look and find ourselves devastated when no one validates our beauty.

I have been able to check off every single one of those thoughts and behaviors at some point in my life. I had my mother's constant reminders not to embarrass her looping in my head like a broken record, along with the punishment and disapproval I got whenever I did something she didn't like. I was so self-conscious about myself and everything I did. I worked overtime to gain everyone's love and approval, while struggling with loving myself and using my voice.

The little girl in me (perhaps like the little girl in you) was invalidated, rejected, and not loved consistently or enough as a child, and those unresolved traumas are a part of me (and perhaps you, too) until we recognize them and work on them (we'll talk about how to do that work throughout this book).

I can't stress to you how important it is to address these sneaky little (or big) feelings now.

If you don't do the work to be stronger and heal from these experiences that laid the foundation for how you feel about yourself, they'll be the barriers to your dreams. Instead of spending time loving yourself, trusting your thoughts, and going after the life you want, you'll be investing energy in worrying about what everyone else thinks about you. You will always be a victim to judgment and the opinions and perceptions of others. You'll get—and stay—caught in the Attention Web, a dark hole of seeking and searching for love, attention, and validation, online and #IRL.

**You'll be waiting around to be chosen, when you should be choosing.**

The truth is, attention and acceptance will come and they will go. You will be popular at times, and at other times you'll feel like not a soul knows your name or cares about who you are. This, ladies, is life.

Love yourself. Be yourself. Choose yourself.

The more you do that, the less you'll be bothered by who doesn't.

## Likes Are Not Life

In this world, it's easy to get caught up in who likes you and who doesn't, especially online. Social media is built on a system of approval—everything is about likes. The more likes you get, the more people notice you. Sometimes likes, or no likes, can equal disappointment and make us feel negatively about ourselves.

Have you ever posted what you just knew was the cutest selfie that you've ever taken in your life, and no one that you cared about liked it? That can make you feel a little down. Or maybe someone made a negative comment to or about you. That definitely can hurt.

I want to help you deal with those feelings, so let me tell you something that you probably already know.

People are mean.

The internet has made it so easy for people to say ugly things about others to intentionally hurt them. Everybody has an opinion about everything, and feels the need to express it. But here's the thing: Only people who don't feel good about themselves go out of their way to hurt other people with their words. Hurt people hurt people.

Even your favorite celebrity isn't exempt. It doesn't matter how beautiful they are, if you look through the comments on one of their images, you'll certainly find ugly comments. Strangers criticize everything from their weight to their hair to their children. Nothing and no one are off-limits.

We live in a culture where bullying is a part of everyday life. The internet makes it easy for people to hurl insults and say hurtful things while hiding behind a fake account. I like to call these people "digital gangsters." There is little to no chance that anyone will go to another's front door and say the things they write. Why? Because they know there is a good chance they'd be punched in the face. The ability to throw shade and hide repercussions is empowering for a coward. So people will talk all kinds of trash when there is no consequence for it.

If someone says something about you, don't let it get to you. You're so much stronger than that. These people don't know you personally. You may have 220 "friends" on social media, but how many of them actually know you? I mean, *really* know you? I am not talking about people who went to school with you, worked with you at a past job, or know you through your parents. These aren't real friends, so their opinions mean nothing to you. You know who you are, and that's all that matters.

Not everything someone says about you is true. Not everyone will like you, and that's okay. Your worth is not determined by what other people think or say about you. What makes us valuable is how we see and feel about ourselves. This is self-love.

## BE YOU: CLUE

*You must love yourself so much that nothing or no one can make you doubt who you are.*

Self-love and self-esteem are an inside job. They are not something someone can give you or pour into you. Yes, people will compliment you and tell you you're beautiful and smart. Or that you're great at something. But there will be a time when you don't get that pat on the back. You will do something you're proud of and no one will even notice. That's life! Or, heaven forbid, they criticize you or try to make you feel like you and your accomplishments are not enough. Everyone may not get it or get you. That is completely okay.

People want you to conform, and will often criticize you for being different. Our culture tells you to compare yourself to others and be just like everyone else to fit in. You always must use labels to identify yourself. You must be this or that. You shouldn't be too weird, you should always suppress yourself or ask a million people what you think you should do, even when you know the right answer deep within. We get addicted to what people think, the labels, the perception. But when we base our self-worth on external factors, it affects us mentally. Even with my crazy childhood, and pretty much raising myself from the age of fourteen, statistics said I should have been pregnant, on drugs, or worse. But instead, I channeled it and bought real estate at age twenty-three, obtained my associate's, bachelor's, and master's degrees, did speaking engagements, and sat on boards of organizations. You get to decide who you are.

Ideally, you don't want or need to be liked and validated by the world. Needing that acceptance leaves you open to abuse, manipulation, and control. If you are always at the mercy of someone's approval, you will never be happy.

Your entire mental state will be determined by the words and thoughts of others. You want to be loved by those who love you for you. You don't want to have to work for love. Just be you, and there will be people who feel it. The first person in line to love you should always be you.

Let's talk about how you do that.

## Pick Yourself First

Unlearning dependency on the justification of others requires us to seek self-validation. As I mentioned before, nothing is wrong with wanting to feel important and liked. We all want to be included. We are inherently made to belong and to have relationships with others. But we also need to build successful, healthy relationships with ourselves. We have to love, know, and honor ourselves. We have to pick ourselves, whether anyone else does or not.

Learn to be your own best friend.

We all want to have people to spend time with, but before you can be a friend to others, or allow them to return the favor, you want to be a good friend to yourself. Spend time alone with yourself to think. Do things you like to do. Write thoughts and ideas in a journal, read about something or someone who inspires you, listen to music, and find a hobby you enjoy. Sometimes you'll want to share what you like with people, or you may want to keep it to yourself for now. You don't need a crowd around you all the time. There will be times when no one can be there for you. That's why loving yourself and being comfortable in your skin are so important. Always pick yourself first.

## Affirm Yourself

The words we whisper to our subconscious mind control 95 percent of our actions. So we have to find ways to fill our minds with positive, motivating thoughts so our bodies will follow. We must change the messaging that we tell ourselves.

Affirmations help us reprogram or unlearn all the things we've believed our entire lives. They help us to focus less on what other people think and more on what we believe about ourselves. Affirmations are words that we can wrap around ourselves like armor to protect us from negativity in the world.

Affirmations are powerful. They hold positive energy and emotions that can quickly shift our attitude about ourselves. Your affirmations don't have to be long, drawn-out statements. They are simply reminders or goals that you repeat to yourself daily.

Try these sample affirmations:
*I am confident and I love how I look.*
*I am smart and I bring joy to myself and other people.*
*I am worthy of the right kind of love.*

Here are tips for creating your affirmations:

- Start all of your affirmations with "I." This makes them personal to you.
- Say your affirmations out loud. Feel the words in your heart as they come out of your mouth.
- Write down your affirmations and place them in your phone so you can easily access them.
- Change your affirmations every four to six months. As you grow, you may have new affirmations to help you focus on what is important to you now.
- Make sure all affirmations are positive. For example, if you want to affirm your beauty, you may say, "I love what I see when I look in the mirror. I see all the beauty of my features. I love my almond eyes, wide nose, cocoa skin, thick lips, and high cheekbones."
- Tie positive emotions to your affirmations. Sprinkle in words that spark joy and gratitude, words that are alive and colorful.
- Speak in the present, not in the past or future. If you are working on a healthier body, say, "I am losing weight now," not "I will lose weight in three weeks." And lastly, believe. For affirmations to work, you must believe in your word wholeheartedly. Just like anything, if you think negatively, nothing will change.

## LET'S THINK ABOUT IT
Take time to think through these questions and write out your thoughts.

1. When you're on social media, how do you feel? Are you inspired, happy, angry, or sad?
2. Why do you think you feel like this?
3. When do you feel left out or not accepted? How does it make you feel?
4. Can you replace the experiences, groups, etc., that make you feel this way with something more positive?
5. If someone else was struggling with not being accepted or liked, or they were needing validation, what advice would you give them? (Hint: You're going to follow this advice yourself.)

## BE YOU: EXTRA CREDIT
Make a list of the things you love most about yourself. Don't hold anything back. Nothing is too big or too small. This is your "I Love Me" List. Come back to it anytime you feel yourself forgetting how amazing you are.

## STAYING SOCIAL MEDIA STRONG
Here are tips to help you stay positive and loving to yourself while you're online:

- Don't conform. If you don't like something, don't feel pressured to go along with the crowd. You don't have

to change yourself to be or do anything just because someone else is posting, sharing, or liking it.
- Post things that are important to you and only you, not just things to get likes. Be you.

## CHAPTER TWO

## Throw Comparison in the Trash

Most women, at some point, have compared themselves to somebody. Anyone who tells you different is not being honest. Now, there are varying degrees of comparison and we may dislike something minor about ourselves and be able to move past it, while other women are far more critical of themselves and spend more time wanting to be or have something else. But comparison is comparison. Whether it's skin, lifestyle, body, or relationship, if you've ever measured yourself up to another woman in some way (and felt bad about what she had that you didn't), you know.

As a child, I constantly compared myself to other girls in the neighborhood. I can admit that, back then, I wanted my hair to be super long, my skin to be lighter, and my lips smaller. I wanted to be a little shorter and curvier like the other girls. In my thirteen-year-old mind, if I could just have one of those things (I wasn't greedy) my life would be easier. I spent so much time wishing I was someone I was not, instead of learning how to appreciate everything I was. But no one was in my life at the time to say, "Tasha, you're beautiful, baby girl!" or better yet, to encourage me to be patient and wait for a few years when I would learn for myself just how beautiful I was. All of the features that I hated so much, including my chocolate-hued skin and my height, are all parts of myself that I absolutely love now. With my short, pixie cut and long, shapely legs that bring me to six feet with my heels, I could easily be the poor man's Naomi Campbell. I'll take it.

So before we move on, let me tell you a couple of things you need to know right now:

1. You're so beautiful, baby girl! (And I mean that.)

2. Whatever you don't like about yourself now, give it time. You will look back on these years and be so thankful for the shape of your body, lips, hair, complexion, and everything else God has given you. You're gorgeous now, but wait until you really learn what to do with everything you have. It *all* comes together, trust me.

As a woman, comparison is an innate reaction—a feeling that comes so naturally that we sometimes don't realize we're side-eying the girl next to us. We feel envy and jealousy creep up (which are completely normal, by the way), and not only are we hating on her, but we're picking ourselves apart.

We compare our looks to other women all the time. Whether we are flipping through pages of a magazine, watching television, walking down the street, or scrolling on social media, there is bound to be somebody who we think has a better body or a prettier face. Or maybe it's not a physical feature. We compare our grades and talents too. If we play guitar and we're in a band with somebody who plays too, we immediately compare our skill level to theirs. We see them as a benchmark to decide if we measure up. You may think there is someone in your class who sings or writes better than you. That's all about comparison, and it causes us to quickly forget how amazing and wonderful we are since we're so focused on what the next woman is doing.

In today's culture where technology is everywhere, it's almost impossible not to compare and measure yourself to someone else's standard. We have become a culture obsessed with comparison. But what is so interesting about it is that the image of the women that we admire so much is often completely fabricated, or at least significantly enhanced. What we think is reality is really a filtered version of the truth.

Do you know how much effort it takes for her to get that #nofilter lighting to hit her cheekbones just right? Do you know how many makeup products it takes to create that "natural," fresh-faced glow? How many selfies it takes for your favorite celebrity to get that perfect pose? (One reality star admits that she takes two hundred selfies to get the one picture that she posts on social media.) So nothing is as effortless as it looks. And even if she does know her angles well and can take a great photo, so can you.

We all have something we can own, and that makes us stunning and special. Our job is to find out what that is. The next woman has hers. You just need to discover yours.

## Everything Is not for Everybody

One Saturday morning, I woke up and decided this was the day that I wanted a weave. My short, cute cut was perfect for me, and I always got lots of compliments on how good it looked. But for some reason, I convinced myself that my natural (well, relaxed, but weave-free) hair was not going to cut it anymore. I had visions of ponytails and high buns and spiral curls. I was ready.

I pulled out my laptop and went to the University of Everything—YouTube. I sat in the middle of my bed for hours, watching videos on how to install weaves. Curtains drawn, hunched over my computer all day, I was determined to figure that thing out. With my hair standing on the top of my head, wearing a tank top and shorts, I looked more like one of the troll dolls than I did the beauties I saw online. I am not sure I even came out of that room to eat. Heck, after watching what felt like a thousand hours of videos, I was practically a cosmetologist.

Needle and thread in hand, I got to work. After three hours of turning my head into a pincushion from sticking that needle into my scalp enough times, I was a hot mess. I mean a don't-tell-nobody-we-friends, I-can't-be-seen-outside mess. I couldn't be seen going out of the house like that. After all, I was someone's mother. I gave up. I knew sewing bundles into my head was not for me.

A week or so later, I went into a salon and had a professional install a weave. Done right, it looked great on me, and for that time, it made me feel good. But once I took it out (which wasn't long after), I realized it wasn't just the technique of installing hair that I was determined to learn. I was chasing someone else's standard of beauty.

## Social Media
### A World Where You Can Be Who You Want To Be

Social media can stir up all kinds of crazy comparisons. With access to so many people so easily, you can find yourself caught up in constantly comparing yourself to others. From stacking yourself up against the girls you went to kindergarten with to your eighth-grade prom date's ex-girlfriend, social media can be a rabbit hole of useless research and comparing yourself to people who just don't matter in your life. Or people who aren't even real.

One gift and curse of social media is that anyone can be anything at any time. Pictures can be filtered and Photoshopped. Toxic relationships can be happy, loving, and all smiles. Shy people can be adventurous, confident, and outgoing. (Have you ever seen someone online who posts the funniest memes, the quickest clapbacks, and the most frequent comments on everyone's pictures, but in person they are boring as hell, hardly speak, and are socially awkward?) Behind the computer screen, you can mix fantasy with the truth. No one can ever know what we truly think or feel. We can hide and belong and be validated. We can be whoever we want to be.

The problem with creating a fake online personality is that you have to keep up with it. If all you post are pictures of a beautiful, perfect life filled with pretty places and expensive dinners, that's what people will expect. You are getting attention and you fall in love with it, and you want to keep the validation coming. So guess what happens? You're spending every dollar you make on new things to keep up the perception. But eventually, it starts to feel hard. What if you run out of money and can't afford the lifestyle anymore? Or what if you can afford it, but partying and posing for pictures to post just doesn't make you happy anymore? Now you feel stuck in a fake version of yourself with no way out.

You don't want to pretend to be someone you're not, or pretend to enjoy what doesn't truly make you happy in order to impress strangers. Not today, not ever. No one wants to live with that kind of stress, regardless of how easy they make it look.

At times, social media can be like a mirage of water in the desert. We watch people with lives that we think we want, and spend hours wishing we could walk in their shoes. But we have to remember that we're only seeing a fraction of those lives.

People rarely put their unhappy moments on these platforms—it's only the good images. We see the beach pictures, the groups of posing friends, affectionate couple shots, and selfies with happy eyes and slightly parted lips in a beam of good lighting. Later, we see the happy engagements, stunning weddings, adorable baby announcements, and expensive-looking vacations. Everybody has times when life doesn't look like it belongs in a magazine or on a reality show. We all go through bad days, and the people who you watch and love online are no different. So be happy for them, but don't get stuck in the comparison game. They are real people with real lives and real problems—you just aren't seeing those other parts. Studies show there is a correlation between social media and depression because of how much people compare themselves to others and lose sight of their greatness and blessings.

Comparison robs us of our true, unique value.

Remember you are uniquely made. When you do, the pressure to compare yourself becomes nonexistent. We all live on this earth together and we are all connected through our souls, but no two souls and persons are the same. I am me and you are you. Funny right? But believe me, it's true. We all have something extraordinary about ourselves, and if we accept our own light, get comfortable with it, and share it, the world would be much less catty.

When we compare ourselves to other people, bit by bit, we're loving them more and loving ourselves less. Think about that. If, over the years, you keep chipping away at your self-esteem a little at a time, it will get to a point when you have nothing left but a spirit full of holes that can never be filled.

Comparing can lead to altering yourself mentally, emotionally, and even physically.

Before I go on, let's talk about that last part.

I'm not against plastic surgery. I refuse to sign any affidavits that say I won't ever get Botox, a breast lift, or anything else. I may need a nip and tuck down the line. However, if I do, it will be to make myself feel better about me, not because of the pressure to be someone I am not. You may make the same choice at some point in life, and it's okay. Just be sure to do it for you. Not to be like someone else, or for a temporary moment of joy and happiness. You don't have to be anyone but yourself—today or twenty years from now.

## Know Yourself, Know Your Worth

Whenever you feel tempted to start comparing yourself to someone else, stop and turn your attention back to yourself. Turn that wasted energy into time spent reminding yourself of everything you have—and everything you are.

When you truly believe in yourself and reconnect with how special you are, you will notice something incredible start to happen. Any nonsense and BS that come your way, you can deflect like Teflon. It's none of your business what other people are doing. If you are so preoccupied with someone else's life, you can't focus on what's right ahead of you. If you are running a race and you keep looking back to see if your competitors are catching up, you are bound to fall.

You will always have competition in life. But you know who your number one contender is? YOU. Your job in this life is to outpace yourself. Keep climbing. Keep improving. Keep striving to make your life better. Be relentless in the pursuit of your dreams.

## BE YOU: CLUE

*Comparison is wasted currency. Invest in yourself. That's where the real worth is.*

## Change If You Really Want To

Believe it or not, comparison can be a good thing. Those feelings of jealousy can be signs that we want more for our lives, and that is normal. Nothing is wrong with seeing someone else's success and wanting equal or better success for yourself. When we flip the feelings, comparison can be the inspiration. But not if you just talk about why you can't have it. You have to decide that you can.

First, you need a plan. Start by asking yourself two important questions and writing down your answers:

1. *What is it about my life that I want to change?*

2. *What areas do I want to grow in?* Is it in culture and experiences? In that case, you may want to seek to understand the world. Is it in your career? Then you want to get clear on your purpose. Or is it in safety and security? To have stability, you may want to have a stable job or home. Any of these things are possible.

Now, you must start working your plan and taking steps toward creating the life you want. Here's how to make moves:

- Pace yourself. If you have more than one area in your life that you want to grow in, decide which one is a priority. Where do you want to make the shift first?
- List the steps on how to get there. Be specific.
- Talk to people about their journey. Ask questions to learn how they got where they are and how you can follow the same path.
- Stay focused on your finish line. (Whenever I decide to change anything important, I ask myself, "What is the consequence if I don't do this?" What will you lose? How will your life stay stuck and the same if you

don't grow in this area? Think about what is important to you.
- Forget the rest. Put all of your other goals aside and focus on this. You don't want to add stress that causes anxiety or a burden that is too heavy to lift. Give yourself permission to breathe. To relax. To rest.
- Be easy on yourself. If you make a mistake along the way, forgive yourself and get back on track.

## Have a Vision

Visualization is a great tool to shift your life. You have to see what you want to be. Close your eyes and envision what you want for your life. Be detailed. Let your body feel what it would feel like if you had what it is you want. Let it play over and over in your mind like your favorite movie.

If it's hard for you to do this with your eyes closed at first, look in the mirror and visualize the person you want to be. Make it real. Be confident. You can become her.

I always had a vision of who I wanted to be. It was always a battle between my current situation and the life I wanted. My vision was fuzzy at the time, but the more I thought about it, the clearer the picture became.

At times, the picture worked just like an old TV. The image would phase in and out, but I held on to it. It was a survival tool that kept me focused on the life I could see for myself as opposed to the one that was in front of me.

You can do the same with your vision. Hold on to it. Make it your reality.

## LET'S THINK ABOUT IT
Take time to think through these questions and write out your thoughts:
1. How can you be the best version of you?
2. Do you know your purpose in life? What is it?

## BE YOU: EXTRA CREDIT
1. Write down three things you are grateful for.
2. Instead of comparing yourself to women you don't know, commit to focusing on building one relationship with someone new who you'd like to get to know.
3. Repeat this affirmation: I am only in competition with myself.

## STAYING SOCIAL MEDIA STRONG
Here's a tip to get away from constant comparison online: Take time away from social media. Detox for at least two days a week. Give yourself time to breathe and focus on your goal and visions without distractions or the temptation to compare yourself to others.

## CHAPTER THREE

## Know You Are More Than A Body

Facebook and Instagram flood our timelines and feeds with images and, let's be honest, a lot of them are of women flaunting their bodies. For some ladies, showcasing their bodies online is their way of promoting body positivity and sending a message to the world that says, "I love my body and I'm proud of it." Many women make a living showing their bodies. I follow several fitness accounts that are run by women who share pictures of their bodies all day, every day.

I use their content as motivation for me to keep exercising and stay focused on my path of a healthier lifestyle. And then some women put their bodies out there for other reasons . . .

This is not about judgment. We all have the right to do

what we want to do, and post what we want to post. But we all can agree that some women and girls are not posting to inspire anyone. Their goal is to feed their egos. They want attention so they can feel better about themselves. These women want to prove to others that they are worthy. Their worthiness comes in the form of likes or favorites. They need validation. This may not be a popular opinion, but deep down we all know it is true.

One Christmas holiday, I was sitting around the table with my younger cousin and his friends. They all were between the ages of sixteen and nineteen. One girl was in the group, and naturally, we struck up a conversation.

We talked about a lot of things that night, including music. She and I started out talking about popular hip-hop artists and songs from the '90s, which was my era. Back then, rap was all about storytelling. I schooled her on my favorite songs and lyrics from the greats of hip-hop, Nas, Biggie, and Jay-Z (full disclosure: I'm from Brooklyn and those men are always everyone's Top Three, with an honorary mention of Tupac). The young lady intelligently expressed her views on why she was a fan of younger, more contemporary artists. She spoke highly of each of them and why she thought they were so good. I was impressed.

In an attempt to prove her theory, she pulled out her phone to show me the new artists that she'd posted about on Instagram. As she scrolled through her feed, I looked over her shoulder and was shocked at what I saw. This girl who was so intelligent and articulate had hundreds of pictures of herself on Instagram, half-naked.

I couldn't help myself. I had to say something.

"You're way too pretty to be showing off your body like that."

I waited for her to shy away from my comment and attempt to quickly change the subject, or give me some excuse.

Her response surprised me. She honestly told me that she put up those pictures so guys and girls can see how good she looks. "I want to inspire people," she added.

After imagining myself literally popping her in the back of her head like an older sister would, I thought it would be best to engage her differently and possibly show another point of view.

When I asked how it made her feel when people didn't like her picture, she said it made her feel bad and corny, and when that happened, she would remove it and replace it with another photo. It was all about peer pressure. She would scroll through her friends' pictures to see what they or other girls were posting, and compare her pictures to theirs. Since they posted provocative, sexy pictures of their bodies, she started doing the same. She said it was like a drug to see how many people liked her pictures.

That made me so sad. We ended the night with me pouring as much positivity into her as possible. I reminded her that she didn't need to inspire anybody with her body, and that there was so much in her mind that she could use. I don't know if all of that sank in. I hope it did. I hope it does. (Hint: That message is for you too.)

In our culture, we focus so much on our bodies and how we look. It consumes us. As women, we are bombarded with images of what is supposed to be the perfect body. We are taught that thin is good, and if you have a slim body and flat stomach, you are the beacon of beauty. In every magazine, newspaper, commercial, or social media advertisement, all you see are representations of skinny girls. So what does that do to our self-image and how we see our own bodies? We believe that anything other than thin is unacceptable.

When the modeling industry decided to put a plus-sized model (in reality, she was by no means plus, she was a size twelve) on the runway, some other models were furious. They thought it was a mockery of the industry where the standard has always been thin. All of us have been brainwashed into thinking that unless a woman is a size six, she does not meet the standard of beauty.

We see this same trend on social media. Skinny women are applauded and praised. The message, "I'm only good if I'm thin," is programmed in our heads. I've seen girls as young as twelve years old posting pictures showing off their bodies, mimicking what they've seen as the standard of beauty.

For a lot of women, sharing their beauty is a daily job. You know the ones. They post several selfies every hour. Each image has a catchy caption that suggests everyone wants to be like them. Now, let's be honest, do you think this person is walking around so full of themselves that they are convinced people want to be like them? No. It's all smoke and mirrors. These posts are misdirected energy in an attempt to validate their existence. This is not to shame anyone, but I do want you to start thinking differently about what you see online. I want you to see that everything is not as it seems. I want you to see the truth.

The truth is that the people behind those pictures may not be as confident as they seem. Those images may be harboring and hiding deep, dark insecurities. That #nofilter is a cover-up for a sad woman who doesn't love herself as much as she should, if at all. Their camera phones may not have caught their behaviors. So many people are coping with insecurities, alcohol, sex, and drugs. Never take a face at face value. You never know what is going on behind that post or a hashtag.

Society would have us believe that women's bodies are objects as opposed to living, breathing entities with feelings, minds, and souls. When you see a female model in a magazine, have you ever noticed that she is usually motionless and not active? The camera angle is almost always positioned to highlight only specific parts of her body, like her hands, eyes, and lips. But in men's magazines, it's different. Those models are usually in action and moving. Their whole body is represented. Not just pieces.

We are whole human beings. You are more than just your lips, or the part of you that the world chooses to focus on. You are more than just a physical body. There is so much more to you than that.

It's important to know that you are perfect just the way we are. I tell this to every young lady I know, including my eight-year-old daughter. I see her give models second looks in magazines and stare two seconds longer than I would like her to. I know she is silently comparing herself to what she sees, and possibly judging herself for what she thinks that girl or woman has that she does not—yet. Whenever I notice her doing it, I always reinforce to her that she is God-made and she is perfect.

You are perfect too.

Despite what you may think, no standard of beauty exists for you to measure up to. You are the standard for yourself. You have the power to be happy just the way you are. Before you compare yourself to others, take a step back and take note of all you have to be grateful for that's more than just superficial looks. You may have legs or arms when others don't. You may have eyes that can see, and hands that can flip the pages of this book. You may not have to worry about how you will find food, you may enjoy good health, and you may have people in your life who care about you. Be thankful for what you have.

Everyone can't be a size two. Now, if you want to change your body to be healthier, do it. I support that all the way. Do it because you are focusing on being a healthier you, not losing weight to be vain or so more people will like you, and definitely not so you can be what you think you're supposed to be.

## Learn to Love You, Flaws and All

None of us are perfect. And we shouldn't be. We are real women, real people, not Barbies who were pieced together in a mold. All of us have flaws and blemishes. They are small cracks in our visual representation where our real beauty (like our confidence) can shine through. And they make us beautiful.

Learning to love your flaws is like writing a love letter to yourself. It says, "It's okay to send kind messages to myself. It's okay not to be perfect." It allows you room to improve and continue to look in the mirror with kind eyes and say, "It's okay. I am okay."

I've learned to love all my flaws and blemishes. I will always love myself more. You should too.

When we look at our bodies (as young girls and when we get older), we often immediately point out what is wrong. *Is my butt too small? What if my thighs were a little bit smaller?* But as we become more self-aware, we find ways to accept those things. If need be, we find ways to work with our flaws and maybe do things that play up our assets and what we love about ourselves so the flaws don't matter to us as much.

The more I worked on my confidence, the more I found out things about my body that were uniquely made just for me. Some would call them deformities, but I thought of them as little evolutions of the human body. I convinced myself I was ahead of the curve. A doctor confirmed that my crooked thumb was a mutation, so I can be a real X-Men character. I stopped seeing it as a flaw that made me self-conscious, and embraced it as a part of me and what made me unique and beautiful. I even talk about it to make people laugh and to start a new conversation with people I've just met. It's one of the things I am known for. And while I spent years being worried about it, the truth is, nobody notices my thumb unless I tell them. That's the thing about our flaws. Far fewer people notice them than we think. I have redefined my image of what a perfect body is for me.

## It's Your Energy, Not Your Exterior

You have an energy deep within you, a light that no filter or flash on a camera phone can alter. This energy is a glow that shines outward. This energy does not need approval from strangers on Instagram or Snapchat Stories or Facebook or Twitter. It's a positive energy that no one can take from you. But you can voluntarily give some of it away. You can allow people to penetrate it when you are comparing yourself to others, discounting and doubting yourself, and focusing more on your body and outward beauty even though they are only a fraction of you. You should be flooding the world with the energy and the light inside of you, not what is on the outside. So you have to protect that energy at all costs.

Every time you feel insecure, your energy dims a little more. You protect it by putting all of that effort into self-awareness. Knowing who you are. Building yourself up. Being confident. This will bring an inner peace that your soul deserves. You will notice that your thoughts are clearer and your decisions are sounder. Nothing will be able to take your energy from you.

Being self-aware is important, so you are not easily swayed. When you're on social media and out in the world, with all of the information and images and others' ideas and opinions being thrown at you, you need to know when, and how, to filter out the noise. When you are online, especially, you have to be intentional with your thoughts and what you allow to enter your spirit.

What you read, watch, and listen to is all digestible. There is some science to the saying, "You are what you think." You are also what you see and hear. The good news is you can rewire your brain to think differently. You can have a positive reaction to every thought you have. The brain is like a muscle. If you change your beliefs, feelings, vision, and actions, your brain will put out more positive thoughts, faster and faster, so that negativity won't have a chance to live inside you and cause chaos.

The same is true for people. Watch out for negative people and be careful not to allow yourself to digest and absorb their energy. Have you ever wondered why, when you're around certain people, you feel drained as if they sucked the life out of you? These people always have an insignificant complaint about what a celebrity is doing, who wronged them, or a depressing story they read or saw on the news. After having a conversation with this person, you feel just a little down, not your jovial self. It's because they pull all of the air out of the room. They are a magnet for depressing, sad information and they have sucked you into their vortex. This is called transference of energy. When you see this person's number pop up on your phone, hit that "Ignore" button. Your voicemail is better at handling these Negative Nikkis. Don't waste your time or your precious energy.

Okay, here's something hard to think about. But it needs to be said. What do you do when you're that person? When you are the one who is consumed with who is doing what and who, and who comments under every gossip blog. You are a complainer. Your thoughts are always negative. You could be the one draining your energy, dimming your light. If this is you, you must start to shift—for yourself and others around you.

First, be honest with yourself. Take responsibility for your decisions and emotions. The truth can be ugly. No one wants to hold up a mirror to themselves and really discover who they are, let alone do the work. In this case, get help.

There is no shame in asking others for feedback. Ask people how they see you. Ask if you can be negative and if they have any reason why they would not want to be around you. This is not easy, but it's necessary. People who you trust will be gentle but honest with you. Receive what they have to say and be honest with yourself.

When you've asked the hard questions and sat still to hear the answers, your true values and beliefs become clear. You can begin to see your strengths and weaknesses and conquer them head-on. The biggest gift is that you learn who you really are and the changes you need to make to become a much better you.

## What's Important to You

Every day, my daughter and I take a walk. As I listen to her talk about her day and the chronicles of the fifth grade, I can always tell what matters to her, and who or what has affected her, based on what she tells me, whether or not she shares all of her feelings. Above everything else she says, I always zero in on that, and when she takes a breath, I ask her to take time to think about one question:

"What is important to you?"

This is my way of encouraging her to think more deeply about herself. I want her to turn down the volume on all of the noise in her head about who said what about her or what she experienced that made her feel something negative about herself. I want her to take time to reflect on who she is, how she sees and defines herself, and how smart, beautiful, and proud she is. These are the qualities that matter most. I am happy to say she does so well with this, and even on days when she's feeling sad, those few minutes center her and clear her head and her spirit of the negativity, bringing her right back to the positive, colorful young woman that she is.

What I share with my daughter is a part of an exercise that I started in my twenties, and that I still use for myself and share with young ladies all the time. I started with making a list of the unique traits and values I wanted to see in myself. None of these things were physical. I only focused on the woman I wanted to be on the inside—confident, strong, loving, and kind—that had nothing to do with my body, how I looked, or the clothes in my closet. I would often ask myself who I wanted to be, and what type of person I wanted to be remembered for. Those are the qualities that made the list.

That's what became important to me.

For as long as I can remember, I have always told people that I live my life like a eulogy versus a résumé. When my life is all said and done, I don't want to be remembered for where I worked or the awards or education I received. Yes, those are part of who I am, but they are such a small part. I am so much more than my career. I want to be described as funny, adventurous, spontaneous, a thinker, compassionate, and loving. So those words also made my list.

I also got help. It took courage, but I swallowed my pride and asked friends and family to describe me in three words. I would see if those words matched up with the better self I was building. We all have blinds spots (like the constant negativity that I mentioned earlier) that we don't see. Those little cracks and spaces that we try to ignore. Don't get me wrong; feedback is hard. None of us want to be criticized or to hear what people think about us (when it's bad). But this is how we grow. More often than not, people shared positive traits with me, so it wasn't all bad. I got reminders of the things I'd overcome, large and small. (If the people you love *only* have negative things to offer you, you may need new friends.)

Once I had my list of words, I wrote each one on a Post-it note and put them everywhere as constant reminders. Those notes were all over my apartment, on my mirror, in my wallet, in my purse, and even in my medicine cabinet. I put them every place I would look at or open daily to keep me focused on the qualities I wanted to nurture, and all the internal things I thought were fantastic about me. These were my important qualities. Those sticky note reminders of the woman I was and the woman I was becoming worked to shift my mind during my darkest times. I am happy to say that I was able to step into the vision of that woman, and now I live it out every day. By focusing on what was important to me, I left little room for negative outside influences or experiences, or people who would drain my energy or try (and fail) to make me feel bad about myself.

I was only focused on what was important to me, the qualities and traits that would contribute to my success and make me a great woman, mother, and friend. And, newsflash, none of those things are my butt and boobs (I am just saying).

Now, I want you to do your work on figuring out what is important to you:

- List the traits and characteristics that you love about yourself. Nothing physical—this is all inner stuff.
- List the traits and characteristics that you may need to work on.
- Ask three friends to describe you in three words. If they offer you negative things, think about how you can be better. Add those new words to your list.
- Write each word on a separate Post-it.
- Stick your notes all over the place and look at them several times a day to remind you of who you are and who you are becoming.

## Become a Judgment-Free Zone

It is important to do a self-awareness scan as you are building a better you, especially when you are on social media. As you are scrolling, check in with yourself. Are you allowing little negative talks to creep in? Are you being unfairly critical of your body or how you look? Are you judging yourself?

It is important that you give yourself room not to be

judged. Give yourself space in your universe to refrain from negative talk and take a moment to observe what is going on. Most times, when we talk negatively to ourselves, it's an exaggeration. Ask yourself, "Is this an accurate assessment of who I am, or am I feeling this way based on what I am seeing right now?" and "Am I exaggerating? Am I really X, Y, or Z?"

Our perceptions of ourselves can easily be swayed by temporary emotions and situations.

If you get in an argument with your boyfriend or a girlfriend and you start to experience negative self-talk based on what was said to or about you, that is a temporary situation. Stop and think about whether your self-talk is true, or if you stretched it out of proportion because of the argument. And then ask yourself, "Does this really matter?" The funny thing is, most of the time, it doesn't.

Before you start changing based on what you're feeling, be sure you are not judging yourself too harshly due to information that may or may not be true. As you are becoming a better you, be easy on yourself. Have patience. A new you won't be built in a day. As you are learning and growing and becoming more aware of yourself, pay attention to all your edges and jagged spots that exist and slowly begin to accept and tolerate all those spaces until they are smoothed out.

The world will give you your fair share of unfair judgment. Don't do that to yourself.

## BE YOU: CLUE

*Judgment is a negative frequency and vibe.*
*You can shake it off, sis.*

## What Really Makes You Beautiful

Your self-esteem and confidence are about more than how you look. Yes, you're pretty. But what else is going on inside of you? Are you loving and caring to your family, friends, and other people? Have you set goals for yourself and created a vision for a beautiful life? These are the important parts of you that matter most. Are you kind to people who can't do anything for you? It's easy to be kind to a mother, father, or sibling, but what about the person who can't offer anything in return? That means you have a heart and love for others. That's all on the inside. And that makes you beautiful.

How we feel about ourselves also makes us beautiful beyond measure. You may look up to several young women online who have a confidence that has nothing to do with their looks. That glow you see is from knowing who and what they are and focusing on what is right about them as opposed to what other people may think is wrong. These women have a vision for their success. They are living their lives as best they can. They are working hard toward the lives they want. They are making choices to accomplish their goals and to be as happy as they can be.

They are picking themselves. So you have to do the same.

Protect your energy and be positive. Work on the inner qualities that are important to you and that matter. Give and receive love. Build relationships. Get motivated and inspired. Post less and live more. That is what a beautiful woman does.

If you become that woman, people will want to scroll, stop, and stare at you too. They will want to know how you can reflect such inner beauty, regardless of your outer beauty.

## LET'S TALK ABOUT IT

Take time to think through these questions and write out your thoughts:

1. How do you see yourself in the mirror when you pass by?
2. What flaws make you uncomfortable?
3. What can you do to become more confident in how you look? Is there anyone you can talk with who can help you?

## BE YOU: EXTRA CREDIT

Every day, take a few minutes to do self-reflection. You don't have to spend a lot of time on it. It could be as simple as walking to the store. Get fresh air and focus on you.

## STAYING SOCIAL MEDIA STRONG

Here's how you can stay body positive and ensure you are positively portraying yourself online.

Not all pictures on social media are a bad thing. There are many tasteful bikini pictures and sexy photos online. If you feel comfortable and what to share a photo of yourself at times, go ahead. But always be mindful of where those images will end up. Once they are on the internet, you can't pull them back. You may be able to delete them, but someone already may have downloaded them, or they may be stored in the site's archives. They are out there forever. That means if you are going for a job interview and the interviewer Googles your name, that picture may pop up. Is that how you want to be perceived? If you may not be proud of it later, then think twice about posting it.

Here is a quick test whenever you want to post something. Ask yourself:

- Why am I posting this?
- Is this for attention?
- Do I want someone I like to notice me?
- If someone I didn't know saw this, what would they think of me?
- Does this photo make me feel proud of myself?

## CHAPTER FOUR

## Never Stop Growing

Self-esteem can be a tricky thing. If you don't have enough of it, you can feel like you are trying to climb an ice mountain with slippery shoes. Too much self-esteem and you're posing everywhere you go like you are Beyoncé with your own wind machine, and your ego is so big that you can't see anything or anyone else around you. In reality, you want to be somewhere on the spectrum. Confident, aware, and always growing.

You never want to get to a place where you think you've reached the pinnacle of success. You can always do more work on yourself. Self-improvement, which fuels your self-esteem, is constant work. Growth gives you a higher goal to reach for every day, whether it's in your grades, your jobs, your relationships, or your self-esteem and self-love.

You don't ever want to see yourself as someone who settles, is good where you are for life, or doesn't see the value and advantage of improving. Keep that drive that makes you feel like you can burst through walls, and don't let it dry up because you feel content where you are. Yes, love yourself as you are, but your number one job in life is to keep striving to be better than you were before.

We've talked a lot about how we can improve our self-image and self-worth that are constantly being challenged on social media. Self-esteem is such a big topic that I want to talk with you about it a bit more, especially those experiences that can affect how we feel about ourselves and what to do about it. Self-esteem is like a plant: for it to grow, you have to water it every day and give it the sunlight of positivity and feeling good about yourself. But along the way, you have to pull some weeds.

It is not easy to look at ourselves. How we feel about ourselves is shaped by experiences and circumstances, some of which we had little to no control over. Our lives are layers, and our self-esteem is buried beneath a lot of stuff. We have to pull back those layers to uncover who we are and why. This process can take a long time. It took years for me to identify with a good picture of my self-worth. I had to be in a place where I was willing to see things that hurt. For example, when I was a young woman, I was in a mentally and emotionally abusive relationship for ten years with an older guy. At the time, I didn't think I was in an abusive relationship. I convinced myself that the hurtful behaviors I endured weren't that big of a deal.

It took time for me to say out loud, "Damn, this is enough. I'm being abused." I had to accept that the situation was not a good one, and that I was damaging myself by staying in it. That is just one of the many experiences in my life that impacted how I saw myself and took a toll on my self-esteem. I had to acknowledge it, and over time, work to undo the damage that had been done. The feelings of unworthiness that were left after that relationship still come up sometimes. That is why it's important to stay aware and keep growing. If I decide that I have done all of the work now that I am grown-up, I would be missing an opportunity to honor my feelings and continue to build up my sense of self-worth. I need to keep building it up because there will always be new experiences around the corner to test me.

When I started a new relationship, it was easy to fall victim to the monster of low self-worth. A quick thought would flash through my mind, wondering if the person thinks I'm enough, smart enough, or if I would make a good wife. Because I am aware, I know where those thoughts and feelings came from. I know the abuse that I suffered caused damage, and my self-worth occasionally took a beating. Many men and women suffer from this. That's why it's important to always do the work and take time to reflect.

I grew up thinking you can endure anything and it didn't matter how people treated you. But I had to unlearn that. I had to develop the tools to build a small fence around myself to protect and build up my self-worth. It's possible to straighten out those dents in your self-worth so you can recover more quickly, or build your fences that protect your self-worth at all costs.

This is what growth is all about.

This process takes time. You won't wake up one day and say, "You know what? I'm the best person in the world and no one can take that from me!" If you will get to that point, you'll stop doing your affirmations and self-reflection work and you'll get over-confident. Then a relationship or an argument or a negative comment will come out of nowhere and take you back a few steps as a valuable reminder that you always have more growing to do. We all fall victim to our self-worth being damaged from time to time. No one is immune to that. But you don't have to stay stuck in that negativity. Stay aware and do your work.

## BE YOU: CLUE

*It ain't what you walk away from, it's what you walk away with. Lessons you need to grow will always come out of any negative situation.*

## See It For What It Is

If you keep running into issues related to your self-esteem, the first step to breaking the cycle and conquering it is to acknowledge that you have a problem. Most people don't realize they even have an issue. Remember how I didn't realize I was in an abusive relationship? If someone would have told me at the time, I would have whipped my head around and looked at everyone else in the room, other than me. My response would have been, "Who me? No way! Stop playing!" I didn't know I had a problem until I was willing to see it.

Your situation may not be as serious as abuse, but you know when something isn't right. If you don't feel good about yourself in any situation or relationship, and it just doesn't sit right with your soul, you know that you need to start looking at the problem and examining how you got there.

Another clue that we have self-esteem work to do is to pay attention to what triggers us online. After you argue with a family member, boyfriend, or co-worker, do you go online to destress but find yourself stressed out even more as you scroll through everyone else's timelines and feeds full of happy pictures? Are you upset about their great jobs, family photos, and engagement shots? This is an indication that you have work to do in your own life and how you feel about yourself.

In real life, those things that make us want to "go off" and, you know, "keep it 100" on someone when they have wronged us are also signs to look for when it comes to our self-worth. You may think you are setting people straight and speaking up for yourself, but are you really? Or are you triggered about something you are insecure about (likely an area where you need to grow) and someone is simply trying to help you see it? Feeling the need to be disrespectful to people who are only trying to help you grow is a sign that you have more work to do.

Our bodies don't lie. Right before you go off of an emotional ledge, how do you feel? Is your neck tense and your tongue hitting the top of your mouth? Do you have a large lump in your throat? Pay attention to what happens in your body. It will tell you what emotions are coming up, and if you listen hard enough, your body will also tell you why you feel how you feel.

## Feel Your Feelings

The next step is to get control of your thoughts and manage your emotions. Start paying attention to what you're thinking, and let yourself hear and feel.

When you're hurt or sad or angry, you need to acknowledge the emotions you are feeling. Don't try to push them down, ignore them, get drunk and party, and act like they don't exist. You can't run or hide from your feelings, and you definitely can't drink, smoke, or anything-else them away. If you try that, when you wake up, the room will be spinning and you will find the problems will be right there waiting for you, perhaps even worse than they were before.

Practice these steps instead:
1. Acknowledge that your feelings are normal and okay.
2. Say how you feel out loud to yourself or someone you trust.
3. Get clear on why you feel the way you feel.
4. Feel your negative emotions. Allow them to move about your body and then allow them to move on.

When you do this enough times, you build resiliency and become immune to the different types of emotions that you feel. They won't knock you off your game for long or make you want to hide under your covers for days. You'll be able to bounce back.

This is not easy work, and it takes time. You will have to do it over and over again to get it right. (This is something I practice daily, so don't worry.)

The work is to get comfortable with being uncomfortable. Be committed to growing, and the discomfort and pain of knowing what's on the other side. Instead of running from discomfort, sit in it. Sit with the feelings. Let them wash over you. Observe your thoughts and feelings. Think of it this way: every time you've experienced disappointment or discomfort, you grew just a little more. There is joy in growth, believe me.

This world will try to tell you differently. Cruel people are out there who enjoy pointing out flaws and inadequacies in others. Look, bad stuff is going to happen. People will wrong you. You will make mistakes and you will get it wrong a lot of the time. But that's life, that's growth, and that's learning a little bit more about you.

## You Got This

Now that you have a clearer idea of what areas you still need to grow in, let's talk about how you manage these emotions while you grow. Here are techniques to try:

**GET STILL.** Quieting your mind is one of the best ways to deal with emotions. You may have noticed that I've mentioned variations of quiet time and self-reflection throughout this book, and that's because I know it works. Life moves fast and we all have a lot to do. Getting to your goals is great, but if we're constantly moving, we miss the opportunity to take in what's going on around us, to feel our feelings, and to deal with them.

Now when I say quiet your mind, I'm not expecting you to sit in the middle of the floor, butt naked, channeling ancient gods. (If that's your thing, no judgment. Do what works for you.) Honestly, quieting your mind is more about finding a quiet spot and just breathing. The thoughts will come and, at first, they will be so fast and furious that it will be hard to keep up. But as time goes on and you practice more, observe the thoughts. If a thought pops in your head, experience it for what it is and let it go. Imagine you are hovering above your thoughts and just let them pass. The trick is to be aware of every emotion, every feeling, in your body. This will take time and you will fail more times than you succeed. But once you get there, it's well worth the wait.

**IGNORE PEOPLE.** No matter how hard you try to be calm and peaceful and embrace your growth, there will always be some jerk who comes to knock you off your square. Nothing makes me angrier than when I'm practicing my Namaste or trying to be still (even if it's just in my head) and some bully comes into my life with negativity. When this happens, you may be tempted to start cursing or to respond in anger. But don't. You can't. Stay in your growth work and walk away. Don't comment on the post. Don't respond to the text. *Nothing.* Focus on you. This is more for you, not them.

**CHANNEL CREATIVITY.** If you encounter a situation that upsets you, write it out in your journal. If you can't journal, maybe capture your thoughts in the Notes section of your phone. When my daughter is having an emotional day, one trick I share with her is to draw out her frustrations. The next time you are upset, try drawing or doodling. There is no expectation that you must be the next Van Gogh, so don't try to be perfect. That would defeat the purpose. You just want enough time to distract yourself, calm down, and be still.

These are only suggestions for ways to create space to look within yourself. You can decide what you need to do. You may want to exercise, call a girlfriend, or take a long bath or shower. These are all ways that you can quiet your mind so you can hear yourself and become more aware of the areas of your life and emotional well-being that will help you to love yourself and focus on your personal growth.

## LET'S TALK ABOUT IT

Take time to think through these questions and write out your thoughts:
1. Do you know your triggers?
2. Can you identify your feelings when something upsets you?
3. Have you learned to manage your emotions? What can you do to calm down faster?

## BE YOU: EXTRA CREDIT

Try a breathing exercise. Sit down and breathe in through your nose. Let your stomach fill with air. Breathe out through your nose to release all negative emotions from your body. Repeat this for three minutes.

Try mindful meditation. Focus your attention on what is happening right now in the moment. Use all five senses (sight, smell, hearing, touch, and taste) to be present.

## STAYING SOCIAL MEDIA STRONG

**Here's how you can focus on your growth online:** This may be hard, but unfollow and unfriend anyone who hinders your growth. People you argue with constantly, exes, bad friends, all of them. Block and move on.

## CHAPTER FIVE

## Don't Do Life Alone

They say you are the sum of the five people you are around the most. If that is true (which it usually is) what do your five say about you?

When you think about your current friends, how do you feel about them? Be honest. Are these people truly your friends? Do they have your best interests at heart? Are they encouraging and kind to you? Are they adding value to your life, or are they just taking up space?

I've had most of my friends since junior high school. We clicked, and I never looked back. Three of the women around me are my greatest allies and accountability partners. Together, we learned the highs and lows of being women. We have done life together, including breakups, heartaches, marriages, births, graduations, first homes, new jobs, layoffs, and firings. It's been thirty years and we still talk every morning. We discuss how to raise our kids and who's getting on our nerves at work, and we vent about our spouses. Despite everything we've gone through in life, we support each other and we learn from each other. We encourage each other to live our best lives.

I believe that our bond as friends is stronger because we all wanted more for ourselves and each other. Although we were raised in the hood, we all knew we wouldn't stay there. It's what we talked about every day. We strategized all day, every day. Our conversations were focused on how the game was played, how we were going to beat it, and how to navigate it. When we did fall, we created plans for how to get back up. My tribe does not consist of small-minded people with small thoughts. It consists of go-getters, women who are about that life of success, growth, and happiness.

We all need a tribe of women to love us and support our growth. Online relationships are great, but there is nothing like the real thing. You need girls who can reach out and touch you, and you can do the same for them.

## Clean Your House of Friends

We're going to talk about what to look for in a friend and a tribe, but to recognize what a good friend is, you first have to know what she is ***not***. When we've known people for a long time, it can be hard to see them clearly. We may not recognize if they do or say hurtful things. If we do see it, we may feel inclined to give them the benefit of the doubt. If we don't love ourselves enough, we may hold on to friends who aren't good to us, out of fear that we won't find people who will be good to us and who know us well and who will keep our secrets. We are scared to be alone, and sometimes we think we won't find true friends to hang out and do life with.

That is a lie.

You do not want anyone in your life who isn't good for you. It does not matter how long you've known them or what they have done for you in the past. You have a right to end relationships that are toxic with people who are negative and consistently hurt you. Real friends don't do that. If you have girls around you who need to go, let them.

## BE YOU: CLUE

*Always, always trust your feelings to tell you who should stay or go in your life.*

If you are asking yourself what to look for in a good friend, here are things to think about:

- She won't gossip about you behind your back.
- She won't tell your secrets.

- She will always be honest with you and give you feedback in love.
- She will do what she says she will do, so you can count on her.
- She will be happy for you when good things happen to and for you.
- She won't betray you.
- She will be loyal.
- She will be willing to say she's sorry when she's wrong.
- She won't let you do anything that will hurt you—today or twenty years from now.
- She will love you for you, regardless of what you have or what you can give.
- She will not judge you.
- She will support you in whatever positive changes you decide to make in your life.

All of the women around me have always checked each of the characteristics on this list. As I've gotten older, I've realized that in addition to supporting and loving each other, we all share one important thing, and that is thinking big. You don't want to surround yourself with small thinkers. Small thinkers are dream killers. Our mantra (or maybe it was just mine) is, "If you hang around nine broke people, I guarantee you will be the tenth." You want to be around people who have big ideas. So big that they sound outrageous. You want to hang with people who live on the fringe of being normal. Normal is boring. Conforming is boring. You want people who you can bounce new, crazy ideas off of and they can do the same for you. You are only limited by your imagination, so why be around people who want to put limits on you?

## Build Your Support Circle

If you're reading this and thinking, "I don't know any people like that. I don't know where to find them," trust me, you can. If you can find that cute sweater online that you searched high and low for, you can find a new pair of friends. Go where they are. If you want to open a business, find a workshop for entrepreneurs. If you like art, then go to a class or a museum.

Put in the work to be where they are. Ask the universe for guidance to people you need in your life, and make it your daily affirmation that you find these people. You only want people around you with good vibes!

Social media is great for connecting you with other people who think like you do. You even can find someone in your tribe who you may never have met before. If you find someone online who you admire and they spark your attention, reach out and tell her that you like what she does. You never know where that conversation may lead.

You want at least three to five people in your tribe who make you feel like you are unstoppable. Or women who are so much on top of their game that they inspire you to step your game up. Sometimes these will be friends, and other times, family.

Here is my recommendation for the five types of people you need in your life:

**THE CHEERLEADER.** This is the person who no matter what you do, they always tell you, "Good job!" They are first in line to congratulate you, and stay after everyone else has left the party to remind you how awesome you are, and may even help clean up. You often serve as their inspiration, and they are not jealous when you win. They are sympathetic to your needs.

For a lot of us, this person is our mother, or a mother-like figure. Moms have the great ability to make you feel wonderful, even if you are wearing an outfit that looks run down. You can have on the most hideous thing in your closet, and your mother will hype you up with, "Oh is that new?" "It looks great! Turn around let me see you. Walk for me!" as you strut around the kitchen. You feel like Wonder Woman by the time she finishes loving on you.

However, be wary of too much from the Cheerleader. We all know that people like this are the reason why can't-hold-a-tune people show up to the first round of American Idol. Someone told them they sound like Whitney Houston or Beyoncé, not wanting to tell them the truth. So accept the Cheerleader's compliments, but don't let them go to your head.

**THE WISDOM WHISPERER.** These people have lived a few years and may have it all figured out. They are usually your elders. Think Grandma, your older Aunty, and the great-uncle. Their advice is usually harsh since, at their age, they've earned the right to say it without a filter or have experienced enough to know not to sugarcoat it so you will feel better about yourself. These people in your tribe have seen it, been there, and done that.

Wisdom Whisperers live by the adage, "When you know better, you'll do better." They may not have all the answers and things may have been done differently in their time, but the basic blueprint remains the same. They are the ones who give you a comforting hug, and may not have a comment about everything. But you know through their eyes they understand everything you are going through. They know defeat, joy, and loss because they've experienced them many times over. Most lessons come through their preparation of a meal. Or you may catch a phrase that they say over and over. But most importantly, their biggest lesson is their life.

**THE ACCESS GETTERS.** I love access getters. I refer to these people as the information highway. Have you ever met someone who, regardless of what you want to do, they can tell you how to do it? They will tell you who to get the information from and they will walk you right to the front door to make sure that person helps you.

Access Getters are the ones who invite you to the best events. Not the parties at the clubs, but to networking events. They tend to know everyone. When you walk through the door with them, it's like being on the arm of your favorite rapper at the Grammys. They are always willing to bring your name up to people to let them know what you are working on. They endorse you. They spend a lot of time listening to your ideas and helping you fine-tune them so they can be just right. They will research things before you can finish your sentence. They always are willing to support you, however they can.

Note that this person does not need to be doing exactly what you are doing—they just need to be a few steps ahead of you in life. In other words, they may be a little smarter than you. That's okay. We all need the Access Getter in our lives, smarts and all.

**THE HATER.** Hear me out. Everyone needs a secret Hater on their team. This is not someone who sabotages you. That would be downright foolish. The Hater is more of an agitator. If you say "A," they have to say "B." If you say you jumped over the moon, they will tell you they captured the moon and sold it on Flatbush Avenue in Brooklyn for a bucket of fries. The Hater has to one-up you, all the time. They refuse to let you get ahead. But it's only in their minds.

Although you may think this person is an emotional vampire and keep your distance, don't be so quick to write them off. Hater energy can be good energy. Let this person remind you that you're on the right track. They will keep you on your toes. They will give you the extra push that you need.

Now, let me be clear, you should limit your time with this person. Watch them closely. If you find this person is always toxic, then you don't want them on your team. But you need someone who will not tell you, "Yes," and agree with everything you say and do just because you want to hear it. We all need that person who will push back when we need it.

## LET'S TALK ABOUT IT
Take time to think through these questions and write out your thoughts.
1. Who is on your team that adds positivity and value to your life? Who doesn't?
2. Who would you like to add to your tribe and your life?
3. How can you meet those new people?

## BE YOU: EXTRA CREDIT
Look in your cell phone and scroll through the last five people you texted. Identify each person and the value they bring to you. Identify any friends in your tribe and make sure they stretch you.

## STAYING SOCIAL MEDIA STRONG
Here's a tip for building solid, supportive relationships online: Be a cheerleader for your good friends, and for women you like. Comment something positive on their posts. Hype them up! Be the girl and woman you want others to be for you.

## CHAPTER SIX

## Setting Boundaries

You are creating a new version of yourself. New thoughts, new points of view, new habits, new friends. But for all of this to work, you need to set boundaries too.

Boundaries are not a bad thing. Think of them as rules that define how you function with yourself, and especially with other people. Many of us don't have boundaries. You don't know that you need them until you have enough experiences in life that make you realize you need to manage your energy, emotions, and people around you differently.

Boundaries take work to build. There must be a mind shift. Believe me, you don't pop up one morning and say, "Boundaries set, I'm good!" There must be a change in your thinking. You must be okay with setting personal boundaries and not being all things to all people, or allowing everyone and everything to access you when they get ready. You have to accept that you can't be inspired and working from your strengths if you are depleted. You have to realize that boundaries are not about being selfish. They are more about self-love.

My day job is stressful. One minor mistake and it can tarnish my agency's reputation. So for me to be sane, I must set boundaries for my boss, my boyfriend, and even my kid. If I don't, I will go off on people, giving out slaps and lollipops. (Clearly, don't take that advice. I don't want you in jail on my behalf, trying to explain to the judge that I told you to go around slapping people. In your head, maybe, but keep that under wraps.) The point is you need to be okay about making it about you. A boundary for me is taking those mental health days from work, from everyone and everything. Just unplug. I had to learn to allow myself to do that.

We find that boundaries become hard to set and enforce. We tell ourselves a million reasons why we can't do a certain behavior, but when it comes to boundaries that protect our time, we tend to fail more often than we succeed. The fear of missing out on something is one of the main reasons. If I set a boundary that I stay off social media after 9 p.m., am I missing the funny meme or viral video everyone is talking about or the new celebrity gossip or the pictures my friends are posting of all their travels?

This is how we think. We think something will pass us by if we aren't right there to catch it.

But the truth is you will never miss out on anything that is for you. The universe has a funny way of showing us that. No matter what you do or don't do, time still marches on. Contrary to what some people believe, and this may be a shocker to many, time doesn't stop if they are not around. If you don't attend that party because you choose to stay home and work on yourself or your homework or your business, life still happens. People still show up, the party continues, the food will still be eaten. Here's another fact that is equally shocking: there will be another one and another one after that. If you miss this one, you will get a chance to do it again.

We also avoid setting boundaries due to social conditioning. As women, we think we have to be everything to everyone. We are taught from a young age that the more you do for people, the more people will perceive you as a good person. This argument is false. Doing everything for everyone can take an emotional and physical toll that is hard to recover from. You will look up one day, drained, with no accomplished goals and no joy, only to realize you are taking care of everyone else but yourself. And to add insult to injury, you will be doing it on autopilot, saying "Yes" to everything without any good reason. Don't be that woman.

Always remember that boundaries are not about pushing people away; they are just personal rules that you put in place to be sure you are always taking care of yourself.

## A PSA for Mental Health

Boundaries are about your emotional well-being and being the strongest woman possible. This is new to a lot of us. In the black community, for a long time, we never talked about mental health and the importance of taking care of yourself. We thought everything could be taken care of by taking a nap or drinking water. It was Grandma's response to everything. Lose your job, take a nap. Husband cheated, take a nap. Kids acting crazy, take a nap. Life isn't that simple. We go through things. *Real things.* Some of us are suffering from sadness and anxiety, and don't know what to do about it or what it really is. I've had panic attacks that turned into anxiety that became full-blown depression. If I had not sought out help, who knows where I would be.

As we get older, we realize that depression is not a dirty word. It's normal, and a lot of people are dealing with it every day. Anyone can suffer from depression. It doesn't discriminate on gender, class, or race. It's an internal fight and the over-thinking can affect our mental health. We tend to think our mess-ups are abnormal and that sets the course down the rabbit hole. You are not alone. There is nothing bad about you. You just need support.

If you need to talk to someone professionally, do it. Be proud of yourself for getting help. We are all in this thing called life trying to figure it out, and it's not one-size-fits-all. Find what works best for you and no one else.

## Where Do I Start

When setting boundaries, you have to ease into them. I always say the first step is being assertive. Please don't confuse this with being aggressive or "keeping it 100." People often confuse assertiveness with aggressiveness. That is a poor excuse for bad behavior. You don't have to be rude or nasty.

If you've ever had trouble speaking up when someone does something to you that you don't like or that makes you uncomfortable, that's a sign that you don't know how to use your voice. Being more assertive will help with this. As you practice more, you will find it easier to notice those triggers, the little, subtle signs that tell you when you've had enough or when to walk away.

When I am teaching the importance of boundaries and assertiveness to my daughter, I use the lessons that are right in front of her. For example, every time we would go to a restaurant, for some reason (maybe it is the food gods), they never got her order correct. There was always something wrong, even if it was minor. If I am being honest, I know my daughter has an issue with projecting her voice, so sometimes she wasn't speaking clearly or she was mumbling when she gave her order.

Yes, I'm one of those mothers who makes their kids order their food. I do this because kids need to be able to speak to adults with confidence. My mother always said, "When you are asking me for money, you have all the confidence in the world, but when asking someone for something in Target, you magically forget the use of your tongue." What she was pointing out was that I struggled to speak up in front of other people. So I had to teach my daughter to let the waitress or waiter know that her order wasn't correct, with respect and confidence. At first, she used to look at me and choose to eat her meal as opposed to speaking up. When she did that, I had to give her the Mommy Stare (you know, the one that says, "Don't play with me. I'm trying not to embarrass you before I lose my cool." Yep that one).

Slowly she would speak up. Now, I may have created a monster. She gives her order, and with a smile, asks them to repeat it back to her. Most of the time, the servers have no problem with this request, but often, I can see the look on their face that says, "Who is this ten-year-old kid? Lady, check your kid!" I just smile.

Start with the small things. If your order is wrong, say something. If your grade is wrong, or your paycheck has an error on it, speak up. If someone says something offensive, respectively remind them of how you want to be treated. This takes work, but trust me, it gets easier.

## BE YOU: CLUE

Saying "No" is always a final answer that needs no explanation.

## Reclaiming Your Time

From time to time, we all need to take a step back from something that we indulge in just a little more than we should. This could be television, talking on the phone with friends, or socializing too much. If you feel like it's too much, it probably is. Step back and give yourself space. Setting boundaries around time is essential. Time is the only resource that you can never get back. Don't waste too much of it.

Social media is one of those big time-stealers. We can spend countless hours online. The problem is, it prevents us from being present and living in the now. I have been guilty of this when I go to venues or places, and I am so busy taking pictures or snaps that I'm not enjoying the event. I'm not taking the moment all in, with all my senses: sight, sound, smell, touch, and even taste. Intimacy and connection are lost when I let technology and social media become the third wheel.

We are hardwired for connections, and social media scratches the surface of our constant itch to be with someone else. Some psychologists say it provides a need we didn't know we had—the need to be connected to people twenty-four hours a day. It's true. We do want to be connected to people. But social media gives us a false sense of community and connection. We are not really in a relationship if it only exists online. Yes, we can watch someone's live video when they are at an event and get a few nuggets and a glimpse of the experience, but we're not there unless we're in the room. So we have to put our phones down and *live*. The question is, "How?"

We often hear that the prescription for our social media addiction is to get rid of social media altogether and detox from it. Detoxing is a trigger word that sends people into a panic. We tend to label detox as "bad," but I wouldn't necessarily look at it that way. Detoxing could be a form of a boundary, so we know we need to cut back on social media. That is how I recommend approaching it. Set boundaries and limits on the amount of time you spend on social media and where you get online (for example, no Instagram on dates or when you're having dinner with your parents). This is a good start.

Studies show that when you are trying to change a habit and you see the change as something you want to do, and it's intentional, you have a better chance of seeing it through. So if you believe that you don't have enough time to do the things you need to do, ask yourself, "What am I doing with my time?" If your answer is social media, then you have confirmed the problem for yourself, versus just taking my or anyone else's advice.

What works for me when I'm doing a tune-up and reclaiming my time from social media is asking or meditating on a few questions:

- Is this the right time to be on social media?
- Is there something else that takes precedence?
- What am I neglecting if I give up an hour on social

media or any website?
- Does this align with what I'm trying to do?
- Why am I online?

(Whys are big questions for me. I am always asking myself, "Why am I engaging online? Do I want to catch up with a friend? Am I doing research?)

If you have goals, always ask yourself this question: "Does this move me in the direction of trying to complete my goals?" If not, give it up.

None of this is to say that social media is all bad. It does have positive attributes, but absences and occasional breaks from it can increase your productivity, self-awareness, and mental health.

## LET'S TALK ABOUT IT

Take time to think through these questions and write out your thoughts:

1. Who do you need to set boundaries with?
2. Are there other boundaries that you need, like around your time?
3. Why are those boundaries important?

## BE YOU: EXTRA CREDIT

Do research online about boundaries, and practical ways you can start setting better boundaries in your life. Reading and studying information from trained therapists and psychologists will be helpful for you in this area.

## STAYING SOCIAL MEDIA STRONG

Here's a tip to setting better boundaries online:

Online relationships can move fast. You may meet someone you like, and they immediately want provocative pictures of you, they want to know where you live or where you go to school, and they press you for dates. Slow down. Never share personal information about yourself with people you don't know well.

You don't have to allow everyone who is friendly to have access to you. You get to decide when and if you share anything about yourself, or if you want a relationship to go further. Shut people down respectfully and block them permanently if you ever feel uncomfortable.

## CHAPTER SEVEN

## Handle Your Heart with Care

Intimate relationships are such a pivotal part of our lives. The people we love romantically can have such a big influence on how we see and view ourselves, especially in the early phases of life when we are learning more about ourselves as women, learning how to establish boundaries, and creating our own identities. We've talked so much about self-esteem and self-awareness in this book that it's only right to talk about love and relationships too.

While self-love should always be your first love, it is only natural that, at some point, you will want to share your life with someone. Love is a beautiful and fulfilling thing, when it's right. Whether you are casually dating or looking for a more serious, committed relationship, you can run the risk of losing yourself in the process. When we don't know, honor, and love ourselves enough, it can be easy for someone to come into our lives and hurt us far more than they love us. How do we go from falling head over heels in love to sitting across from someone we feel like we barely even know? Someone who devalues and disrespects us? Someone who lies, cheats, or abuses us in some way? Someone who doesn't guard and protect our hearts? Someone who doesn't bring out the best in us the way that real love should? How, you ask? I'll tell you:

1. We don't love ourselves enough.

2. We don't know what love is supposed to look like, so we accept what was offered instead of requiring our partner to meet our standards.

A woman who loves herself will refuse to settle for anything less than what she wants and desires. This applies to any area of her life, including love. It's important to remember that you get to set the rules when it comes to this relationship thing. Know yourself, so you can clearly define how you want and need to be loved. Get clear on what love looks like for you, so when you are considering allowing (or you have already allowed) someone into your life, you know who needs to stay and when to walk away.

## Is It Really Love

"... but I *looooove* him."

I know you've heard yourself saying those words before.

Or you've restrained yourself from rolling your eyes as you listened to a teary-eyed friend give you a long list of reasons why she couldn't leave a guy who was no good for her. When we love someone, we tend to wish they could be different. We want every horrible thing that comes before that "but" to just go away so only the love is left. You love him, and he may, in some way, love you too. But if that love is not what you want or need, then you have a decision to make, Love Bug. And it should be to let that love go, especially when it's toxic.

Most of us have been in a rocky relationship a time or two when we think that no matter what happens, love will keep it together. I hate to tell you this, but loving someone isn't the only reason why you should be with them. You can love people, but that doesn't mean that love is healthy or reciprocal. You want a love that makes you feel secure, is consistent, and supports who you are now and who you are becoming. If a person does not check those boxes, you must evaluate if you are in the right relationship for you.

It can be hard to see the faults of others when we're looking through the lens of love. When we want to hold on, we try to romanticize people and see only their good qualities and ignore the others. It's not to say they aren't good people. They could be sweet, good-looking, and have a perfect smile, but still may not be right for you. Or maybe it's not them, it's you. Maybe you have internal work, healing, and growing to do before you can deeply love anyone else, or you just need to focus on your goals right now and you don't have time for a relationship that demands a lot of time and attention. The point is, relationships are all about timing and energy. I truly believe that we all vibe out frequencies, and it's the same in relationships. When our energies no longer resonate, that usually signals the beginning of the end. You can love a person all you want. When it's time to close that door, it's time.

Learning what love is, and isn't, starts within ourselves.

## Love Is about Give and Take

As women, it can be easy to fall into the trap of becoming the "Gimmie Girl." That's the chick who is so focused on herself and what she needs, that she's lost sight of what she has to offer in a relationship, if anything. (Ouch, that may have hurt. But I am just being honest). When she thinks and talks about love, it's "gimmie this, gimmie that." Time, attention, clothes, money, whatever. She takes far more than she ever gives. For her, love is a laundry list of things that a man does or should do for her.

I don't want you to be that girl.

Believe me, I am an advocate of self-awareness and knowing the value you bring to the table. But love is a two-way street. As easily as you can think of what you want in a partner, you should be able to express what you have to offer. How can you be with someone if you don't know what you can offer or who you are? Are you the best version of you? Are you the "you" you want to be, and the "you" that you're looking for? Do you reflect the person that you want to attract? If not, this is where the work begins. Not on Tinder or Facebook looking for love.

In relationships, we can get into these selfish cycles without even knowing it. We say things like, "I want a person who makes me laugh or smile," thinking that we're asking for good qualities in a person. But what we're saying is that we want someone who entertains us. That is not someone else's job to make you happy. If your partner happens to do something that makes you smile, great. But you can't expect their sole role in the relationship to be managing your happiness. That can be exhausting. Just like everything else about you, you have to control that.

Even a small shift in thinking can turn your desires into positive vibes and put the focus on developing an environment where each partner is helping each other grow. Instead of looking for someone to make you laugh or smile, look for a partner with an amazing sense of humor. Look for a person for who they are and what makes them happy and comfortable in their skin, not what they can do for you.

When you are happy and fulfilled in your life, you become a whole woman who is open to love, rather than an empty woman who is looking for it. A partner cannot fill the spaces in our lives and hearts that we're missing. Are you with this person because of the gaps they can fill? Are you with them in hopes that you won't be lonely? Whether it's to bring joy into your life, someone to take to a cookout, or just a warm body to watch movies with, your relationship should be much more. Love from someone else won't fix you or replace the self-love you don't have. Look for someone who complements you, not completes you. If you don't, you'll be disappointed every time.

I had a great friend who used to say, "Appreciation over expectation." What she meant was that we should be grateful for the nice things that people we love do for and with us. But we don't want to place all these expectations on them and set ourselves up for heartbreak when they're not met. We can begin to see chinks in the armor of the people we love when they fall short of who we think they should be, as opposed to who they are.

Expectation is the mother of thieves. It can steal time, energy, positivity, and love. Expectations are a heavy emotional weight to put on people, and it's hard for someone to feel happy if they're carrying their fragile heart, happiness, and self-esteem in their hands 24/7. It can lead to resentment and anger. It almost always does.

When we have expectations of someone, what we want, deep down, is for that person to do what we want them to do. And that typically backfires. No one wants to be forced to do anything.

We all know the feeling of asking people to do something for us, and when they finally do, there is no satisfaction for us or them. That's because, deep down, we know the act wasn't genuine. The person probably did it just to shut us up!

Express your wants and needs, yes, but don't push too hard. You don't want to force someone to be kind and loving to you, or to invest time and energy in the relationship. You want the person to do those things from the heart. Trust me, love is so much better that way.

Give your partner room to breathe, and to fall short of your needs at times. They're human and, if they love you, they'll want to learn you and how you like to be loved. Let that happen, okay?

## BE YOU: CLUE

*The best love is when two people are free to be exactly who they are.*

### See People for Who They Are

It takes time to get to know people, so try not to fast-forward your relationship. When you spend enough time with someone, there is a vulnerably they can't escape. Eventually, you will see the parts of their soul that they've tucked *wayyyyyy* in the back so no one else could see. And they'll see yours too. That's not a bad thing. Vulnerability, transparency, and trust are a part of every strong relationship.

We want to see people for who they are, and not who they think we want them to be. When we get into relationships, the real people we're with will always show up—

eventually. That means their personalities, their habits, their weaknesses, all of the good, the bad, and the ugly. Especially the ugly.

Chances are, you'll see these things early, particularly those that concern you (also known as red flags). If a person is selfish, they will show you signs by neglecting to ask how your day was or showing any interest in what's happening in your life. If they disregard your time, they'll show you by arriving late for dates, or not arriving at all. These are indicators of a person's true personality that can't hide from you, at least not for long. You just have to be willing to see it.

## Know When to Move On

In my last relationship, I knew with everything in me that he wasn't the one for me. Every bone in my body told me to run and I ignored them. If I had a dollar for every time that voice said, "This isn't for you!" I would be rich. My gut was speaking loud and clear.

I kept asking the universe to give me a sign that I should let him go. What I didn't realize was that the mere fact that I was asking the universe to give me a sign more than once *was the damn sign*. But I didn't get it. I needed what I thought was a clear omen in the sky, something more concrete. I got exactly what I wished for. The first sign was when his ex-girlfriend started sending me emails.

The second sign was when she showed up at my house. The third sign was him insisting that he should be able to maintain a relationship with Crazy Ex while dating me.

Believe it or not, I still didn't want to let him go. I would convince myself that despite all of that, he was a good person. I would repeatedly talk myself out of the sign that I had just begged the universe to show me, and convince myself that he was right for me. To be with this man, I put everything at risk—my safety (who knew what that chick could do?), my emotional well-being, and my self-esteem. Every time I allowed him to hurt me, I was hurting myself. Eventually, I had to say, "Enough is enough," and walk away. That was not a friendship or relationship designed for me.

If any of this sounds familiar to you, I want you to let it go. No relationship is worth your self-esteem or sense of worth. This is not to make anyone feel guilty or judged (we've all made bad decisions when it comes to men) but this is a wake-up call. Listen to your inner voice, the one that's telling you it's time to end this.

Take responsibility for your emotions and your mental state. The only person's thoughts and actions that you have control over are your own. In my past relationships, I would spend hours trying to tap into the minds of men, hoping to figure them out. Did they really love me the way I thought they did, or were they lying? Why did they do this or that? Why did they hurt me? And then the lightbulb went off. It wasn't what they were doing. *It was what I allowed them to do.* Once I took accountability for my actions and sat still with myself, I realized the outcomes were my own. I created this situation by staying in it and by attempting to control someone else's behavior toward me. That's when I knew I was out.

That experience (and a few more after that) taught me valuable lessons. Love yourself. Keep yourself, and don't lose yourself in any relationship. And never try to convince others to treat you well.

When a situation is not what you envisioned, you have the right to end it. No apologies or explanations are necessary.

## Know What You Want

Create a clear picture of what you want in a partner before starting any relationship. This will save you so much heartache and disappointment.

Be honest and also realistic. A partner's place in a relationship is to add value to your life. That can come in the form of encouraging you to dream bigger, teaching you a new skill, or supporting your goals. Good partners are people who have their own interests, and want you to have yours. Ultimately, what you want is to bring out the best in each other.

Partnerships aren't about battling each other trying to get one another to see the other's point of view. They are about respect, honesty, character, and facing challenges in this world together. That is why you want to know the person you're with. You want to know, sooner rather than later, how they will face the tough times. You want someone who can weather the storms when challenges arise. That is how love endures.

So when you start to get past the superficial and think deeply about what you want in a partner, it shifts your focus beyond yourself and makes for a healthier relationship when you find one.

That will come when you're loving you. We are all radio towers, sending out energy and vibrations. The best way to attract that partner is to put out authentic energies and be your true self.

## Keep It to Yourself

We've all done it.

We meet someone special. They like us and we like them back. We want everyone in the world to know it.

We change our relationship status. We make sure the first fifty pics on our feed are all pics of the two of us.

We shout him out on #MCM.

We do too much.

Yes, it's tempting to share our love with everyone. But it can be dangerous. Social media is a public place, which means our private relationships are open to public scrutiny.

That means the ups, the downs, the temporary disagreements, and the long-term breakups are out there for the world to see. What may be an innocent comment from a friend on your post is blown out of proportion. An overly flirty girl in your boyfriend's Messenger may be about her not knowing boundaries, not him.

Social media can break a relationship.

So be careful what you share. The more eyeballs you keep out of your business, the better.

Here are a few social media relationship rules that you may want to incorporate into your relationship:

- Decide how the two of you will share your relationship on social media in a way that makes you both comfortable.
- Try to avoid taking every comment at face value. Just because a girl comments on something he posts, and he acknowledges it nicely, doesn't mean he's cheating on you. Ask before you assume.
- Don't disclose everything that happens in your relationship. Talk to your partner more than you talk to friends, especially when you're upset about something that you feel was done to you. (That goes for online and #IRL.)

## LET'S TALK ABOUT IT

Take time to think through these questions and write out your thoughts:

1. Do you try to change people you date or do you accept them for who they are?
2. Do you find yourself getting jealous easily when your partner interacts with other women, even though you know he is loyal to you?
3. Love is freedom. What do those words mean to you?
4. Have you had an honest conversation with the person you're in a relationship with about what love is for you and them?
5. Do you think you are ready for love right now? Why or why not? If not, what things can you work on to heal and open yourself up?

## BE YOU: EXTRA CREDIT
Write a list of positive attributes about yourself that a partner would appreciate.

## STAYING SOCIAL MEDIA STRONG
Here are a few more tips to maintain and manage love relationships on social media:

**STOP PLAYING SPY.** This is hard for us as women, but don't dig around your partner's social media looking for anything. You may feel tempted to check it several times a day to keep tabs or see who he is talking to. *Don't.* You and your partner may decide to not follow each other at all to avoid disagreements and misunderstandings.

**SPEAK UP.** If your partner does something that hurts you online, like being too flirty with someone or keeping too many pictures up of a past relationship, say something about it. Be calm and express how you feel, along with what you would like for him to do about it.

**DON'T DO ANYTHING ONLINE that you wouldn't do if your partner was standing right there.** If you wouldn't speak to your old boyfriend in front of your ex, you should not be in his DMs.

## CHAPTER EIGHT

# Setting the Right Goals to Be a Better You

I know we've already done work toward changes you'd like to make, but now it's time to talk about your big goals. All of this was in vain, the reading and the visualizing and the clearing out of all that internal stuff and relationships that keep you from being great—if you are not going to do anything about it. If you are going to talk about it, be about it.

It's time to shift from talking to doing.

Goals that keep us moving toward the bigger vision for our lives are important since they dictate our lives, the decisions we make, where we spend our time, and with whom. When we don't consciously choose how we spend our time, it is so easy to get caught up in somebody else's life on social media, gossip, blogs, and things and people who don't matter. You will find it so much easier to put down your phone instead of spending hours on Instagram when you know you have goals to get to and things to accomplish to make your life better and your dreams happen.

Focus your time and energy in the right place and your life will quickly start to look different.

When it comes to setting goals for your life, don't think small. You want to set goals so big that it will take a different version of yourself to reach them. If you want more, you have to become more.

To achieve anything, you need a plan. Goals need an action plan. The only way to take this big thing down is to do it one manageable step at a time.

Let's do this!

**BE SPECIFIC.** You want goals that are strong and not vague. If they feel weak and negotiable to you, you will just blow over them.

A weak goal sounds like:

*I will take a break from social media.*

Well, there isn't much to that. That's like saying "I like breakfast." Add a little detail and accountability to that.

A strong, specific goal (The Remix):

*I will take a break from social media from the hours of 3 p.m. to 9 p.m.*

Do you see the difference? With the stronger version, you can measure it. You can see if you are on track and if you're making progress. Being clear on how you intend to achieve the goal shows you are serious and that you want to make sure you achieve an outcome.

**SET A DATE.** Give yourself a due date. Be clear about when you want to complete your goals. They shouldn't be open-ended timelines that continue over years. Without a timeline, goals are just dreams or wishes. Knowing a time frame will pinpoint exactly when you should reach your finish line so you can get there and move onto the next thing. Having goals that just continue into the abyss does nothing for the bigger picture you are trying to achieve.

**BE RELENTLESS.** Your goals are like birthing a baby. They are a part of you. You have to nurture them. Feed them. Make them your number one priority. You need to breathe, eat, and sleep your goals. You should have them on your phone or written down so you can read them daily. Writing your goals down allows you to commit them to memory.

**TELL EVERYBODY.** One exercise I like to do when pursuing my goals is telling everyone. If you tell everyone what you're aiming for, people will ask you the status of your project. Even your haters can get in on this. They don't think you'll do it, so let them keep asking. Let them punch holes in every part of the plan. This will keep you on your toes. Prove them wrong.

**GET IN A CIRCLE OF WINNERS.** Execution is contagious energy, so get around people so dope, you need to step it up. People who are achieving their goals, and doing it so well that they make you want to tiptoe around your circle. Let them stretch you.

You may feel a little bit of envy, and that's great. Use that energy as motivation. Nothing is wrong with friendly competition. It makes one want to do more. You need to be comfortable with being uncomfortable. You need to be in unfamiliar spaces. When you're comfortable, you're not learning and growing. Nothing good can happen when you are stagnant. They always say, "Pain is the greatest motivator," so you need to be around people who are going to push you.

One day, my nephew came to me about a business idea he wanted to explore. Full disclosure, he has dabbled in other endeavors before, and got in as quickly as he got out. But I always told him that to learn anything, you must fail and fail fast, so you can learn and recover. He knows he can come to me to weigh out his ideas. I am in his judgment-free zone.

He started complaining to me about people trying to talk him out of his dream. We'd talked about this many times before. I had to give him an analogy that I knew he'd get.

"Look, your business is a new puppy that someone brings home. Initially, you put the puppy in the cage, so it doesn't crap all over the house. But eventually, the puppy will outgrow that cage. That's how you must look at the people around you. Your business ideas and the things you are trying to do have outgrown the people you are around."

He got it right away.

Everything adapts to its environment and evolves. When you are no longer getting what you need from your relationships, you've outgrown them. It's time to get into a space where you can grow.

STUDY. For anything you want to learn, you can find a tool to teach you. Find books, videos, and podcasts to feed your mind and get the knowledge you need to succeed.

## BE YOU: CLUE

*Goals without a plan are just wishes and dreams.*

## LET'S TALK ABOUT IT

Take time to think through these questions and write out your thoughts:

1. Are your goals small enough and achievable that you can measure your progress?
2. Do you have someone who can hold you accountable to your goals? Who are they? How will you bring them into your plan?
3. What goal are you most excited about achieving? Why?

## BE YOU: EXTRA CREDIT

Every night, before bed, plan out the following day. Know what you need to do, and be sure you always leave room for working your plan toward your goals. When you get up, work that list without distractions. Also, use your phone to set daily reminders for your goals.

## STAYING SOCIAL MEDIA STRONG

Here's a tip to stay focused on your goals online: Once you decide which goals you want to focus on, clean up your social media pages and feeds so you're primarily following people who inspire you with information to reach those goals. They may be on a journey just like you, and as they learn and share, you'll be able to apply that information to your own life.

## CHAPTER NINE

## Change for the Better—and Forever

Shifting our lives for the better, in any way, is not easy. Change is one of the hardest things to do. Your mind will give you a thousand reasons why you can't do it. Your job is to give it a thousand more reasons why you can.

You won't know where to start. You will get distracted, disillusioned, and even talk yourself out of changing altogether. That's where discipline and an action plan come into play. But first, you need to figure out your WHY.

Why is this change important to you?

Why do you want this more than anything else?

Why do you have to do this now?

Once you can answer these questions and shift your focus to the things you want, your attitude will immediately follow. Everything we've talked about in this book, from learning who you are to setting goals to building new relationships, all starts with understanding what you want and why.

Next, you need to decide to change. The act of making a decision and declaring it is powerful. It's the pathway to rewiring your brain to become obsessed with the thing you want. When you want something, it kicks your mind into survival mode, which is important because your body is not designed to succeed, it's designed to survive.

Think about a caveman in the prehistoric days. He knew that he had one goal every day when he got up. Stay alive and not get eaten by some huge, wild animal. He had to survive. Our genetic makeup is the same. Over time, we've been taught to seek success and go after things because we want them, not because we need them. But when you want radical change, that is the shift you need to happen. Decide that you *need* to be different, and you will.

I always tell my daughter that we don't grow if we aren't challenged. While we tend to shy away from doing hard things, it's the space where we thrive. If you look back on every breakup, job loss, or death you've experienced, you'll see that you came out much stronger on the other side of that pain. You didn't think you would or could, but you did. But that is the thing—you can't see it while you're in it. It's not until you are further down the road that you can look back and see how far you've come.

Now let's get to working that action plan. Follow these tips to get going and stay moving so you will reach your dreams and goals:

**HAVE A MISSION AND VISION FOR YOUR LIFE.** Sit down and think about the life you want. Nothing is too big or out of reach. Where do you want to live, what type of career do you want, where do you want to go to school, who do you want to meet? These are all important. Write all of this out so you can align your goals accordingly.

**SET SPECIFIC GOALS TO COMPLETE.** We talked about this in the last chapter, but goal-setting is so important for your life that I want to reiterate it.

You need specific goals to know if you're moving in the right direction. "I want to lose weight" or "I want good grades" are not the same as "I want to lose ten pounds in three months" or "I want to get an 'A' in Chemistry." Get clear and know exactly what you want.

If you have trouble creating your specific goals, that is okay. You may be staring at a blank sheet of paper for a long time and nothing will come out at first, but that is part of the process.

Once you have goals in mind, write them down. Record them on your phone if you have to. Get them out. And then look at them every day. You won't notice, but your goals and intentions will become a part of you. Your plan becomes the strategy that guides your life. The trick to this is to never lose sight of what you're striving for.

**MAKE THEM ACHIEVABLE.** I'm a huge proponent of setting goals so big that you must become an entirely different person to achieve them. But we also must be smart and create plans and small steps to achieve these goals. Your goals should be realistic and reachable, or there is no sense in setting them.

Commit to yourself. Make a commitment to yourself (in writing!) that you will stick to your plan to reach your goals, no matter what. There is no accountability partner in this step; this is personal to you. This is about you and your thoughts. Ask yourself, "What do I want from me?" Set your mind to it and do it.

Control your thoughts. Did you know that every thought you have is shaping your life and your destiny? To change your life, you must get out of your own way and out of your head. Pay attention to your thoughts and how your body reacts when negative thoughts take the driver's seat. Watch how your body tenses up, your jaw clinches, and your fists ball up. These are signs you are thinking about something that isn't serving you, is a distraction, and is pushing your mind in the opposite direction of where you want to go. When a negative thought comes at you, clear it out, fast. Your thought patterns control your emotions and your physical energy. Your health—emotional, mental, and physical—has to be your priority if you want to win.

Control your environment. What you see and hear is just as important as what you think. Those factors are big influences on your thought life. Have you ever argued with someone first thing in the morning and it sets the tone for the whole day? Everything that happens after that annoys you, from the sound of someone's voice, crowds, and even people laughing. If you know that someone irritates you, stay away from them. If someone's posts on social media offend you or trigger negative thoughts or emotions, unfollow or unfriend.

**BE RELENTLESS ABOUT IT.** When I'm fixated on a goal, I think about it every day. I eat, meditate, sing, think, hum, and breathe my goal. I consume myself with it. I run through every possible obstacle and roadblock in my mind so I can avoid or handle it when it comes. I see my goals in 3D, from all angles. Do the same and watch how much harder you work for them. Keep your eyes on the prize. Challenges and hard stops will happen, but always keep the vision in front of you.

**WORK FOR IT.** Now faith without works is dead. You just can't dream and have a vision and then what you want magically appears. Don't believe anyone who says that goals will fall into place without hard work and even failure. You have to work like you've never worked before. Here is the thing: the reward comes from what is difficult, not what is easy. You'll know you're doing the work when it's challenging. When you feel like giving up, you know you are on the right track.

**Do something every day.** Small steps are still steps. Work toward your goal every day. If you're working toward a healthier body, you could do ten crunches and one full sit-up every day. If you want to find a mentor, you could send a DM to a woman each day until you find the right one. Those small steps add up. Build slowly if you have to. Just keep doing and moving.

**Reflect on what you've done and how far you've come.** Always track every step you take toward your goal. If you do this, believe me, you will look back and notice that you've come a long way without realizing it. Check in on your progress at least weekly or monthly. Note how you feel. Does it feel right in your gut? Do you feel a sense of pride and accomplishment? Good. Hold on to that.

If you are like me and you like checking things off, a to-do list can be helpful. List all of your goals and check each one off when you achieve it. It brings satisfaction to check off a task on the list, regardless of how small it is. A little accomplishment makes us feel good. It's like the look you have on your face when the waiter walks up with your food. You just feel the happiness engulf your body. Getting things done and knocking down goals should make you happy. Set up a system so you can see where you are and feel that happy feeling of accomplishment regularly.

**Celebrate along the way.** Remember there is success in the journey. Often, we get so caught up in looking at the result (which isn't a bad thing), that we forget there is also success along the way. Take time to celebrate all of your victories. You'll experience days when you don't want to do the work. You'll have no energy and feel the pressure of not having enough hours in the day to get it all done. You'll feel like it's impossible to mentally pull it together.

Keep up your momentum and celebrate along the way. The celebrations are the fuel in your tank. That's where your drive and beliefs come from. Never let your tank get empty from just working and not taking brief moments to pat yourself on the back.

**LEAVE ROOM FOR CHANGE.** When you know this is your plan, it moves just like water. It's fluid, so you will update it, add to it, and remove parts of it. You want your plan to remain flux so you can see what's working and what's not, and adjust accordingly. Flexibility decreases frustration. Shifting at times doesn't mean you're not committed—it just may mean you hit a dead end and now you have to change routes to get to your destination. It's okay.

You got this!

## LET'S TALK ABOUT IT

Take time to think through these questions and write out your thoughts:

1. What would your life look like if you achieved your goals? How would you feel?

2. What are the consequences of not achieving your goals? What will you lose out on?

## BE YOU: EXTRA CREDIT

Create a mission statement for your life. Write it down. Example: *My life is full of happiness, health, and joy. I am here to live out my dreams of becoming a professional artist, and with my talent, I will provide a good life for myself, my family, and others.*

## STAYING SOCIAL MEDIA STRONG

Remember that social media is not your public journal. You may want to share positive progress at times, but that is not where you go to release all of your emotions. Try to keep most of your day-to-day emotions (as well as your frustrations) to yourself and in offline conversations with close friends.

## CONCLUSION

Dear Lady Bug,

You made it to the end of this book! I am so proud of you, and you should be proud of yourself. We talked about tough things and started doing hard work. You should have a journal full of notes, and ideas around ways to change your life, to feel better about things that may be stressing you, and plans to become a better you.

Know that this journey is not an easy one. No guidebook exists that defines what is right or wrong. No video that provides step-by-step instructions on how you should live and grow. It's all done by trial and error. What I know for sure is that you will make mistakes, and that is okay. You will get it wrong more times than not, and that is okay too. You will doubt yourself and at times you will feel alone. That is definitely okay. There are always people in this world who love you and care about you. When you need people, find them. When you need help, ask for it.

What I know for sure is there is a bright light waiting to light up your path. That light is within you. Notice I said *you*. You are in control of your life and your path ahead. It's okay not to fit in or to follow the crowd. It may take time to get comfortable in your skin and find your voice. Just be sure that wherever you go and whoever you meet, online or IRL, stay true to yourself in the process. Always speak your truth and tell your story in the way only you can.

I hope you feel encouraged and inspired by the woman you are, and who you will be. You can feel good about your qualities. You are amazing. You are beautiful. You are talented and gifted in so many ways. You are valuable to people in your life and in the world. You have so much to give.

My wish for you, Lady Bug, is that you light up the way! When you fail, fail fast so you can learn, grow, and gain more experience. Laugh hard, cry loud, seek support, and dance like no one is watching.

Oh, and one more thing, always, always BE YOU, NO FILTER!

# ABOUT THE AUTHOR

Latasha Blackmond, MPA is the President and CEO of Blackmond Digital Media. A Maryland based social media and SEO consulting company. With over 20 years of experience as a communications expert for federal and state organizations, Latasha found herself increasingly interested in social media and its impact on young women. After years of research and personal interviews she decided to put these discussions and her own experiences in a book.

Latasha Blackmond an adrenaline junkie who comes alive in the skies, and when she isn't writing, you can find her scouting out new adventures such as skydiving or learning to fly airplanes.

A native of Brooklyn, New York, Latasha resides in Owings Mills, Maryland with her daughter.

Made in the USA
Middletown, DE
17 October 2023

40988324R00071